COGNITIO HUMANITAS RECONCILIATIO

The Honourable

JAMES K. BARTLEMAN

Out of Muskoka

James Bartleman

PENUMBRA PRESS

Identity isn't given once and for all; it is built up and changes throughout a person's lifetime.
— *Amin Malouf*

Out

of

Muskoka

James Bartleman

PENUMBRA PRESS

This is a first edition published by Penumbra Press. Printed in Canada.

The Publisher thanks Logan Atkinson and Patricia Marsden-Dole for editorial consultation, and Douglas Campbell for copy editing the manuscript. Cover design is by MORRgraphics Inc. Author photo on the inside flap is by Studio von du Long. Back cover photo is by Philippe Landreville.

NATIONAL LIBRARY OF CANADA CATALOGUING IN PUBLICATION

Bartleman, James, 1939-
    Out of Muskoka / James Bartleman.
Includes bibliographical references.
ISBN 1-894131-31-2
    1. Bartleman, James, 1939-. 2. Lieutenant governors--Ontario--Biography. 3. Ambassadors--Canada--Biography. 4. Ojibwa Indians--Ontario--Biography. I. Title.
FC636.B37A3 2002   971.064'092   C2002-904201-1
F1034.3.B37A3 2002

The publisher gratefully acknowledges the Canada Council for the Arts and the Ontario Arts Council for supporting Penumbra Press's publishing programme. The publisher further acknowledges the financial support of the Government of Canada through the Book Publishing Industry Development Program (BPIDP) for our publishing activities.

For Marie-Jeanne

To my parents, who sacrificed themselves for their children. To my children — Anne-Pascale, Laurent, and Alain — for pretending to listen attentively to accounts of my early life in Muskoka. And to Sandra Black, Arthur Blanchette, Alan Bowker, Patricia Marsden-Dole, Richard Gorham, Carole Jerome, John Mundy, Jerry Mahon, Arthur Menzies, Nancy Muse, and Micheline Roche: for your help and encouragement.

Contents

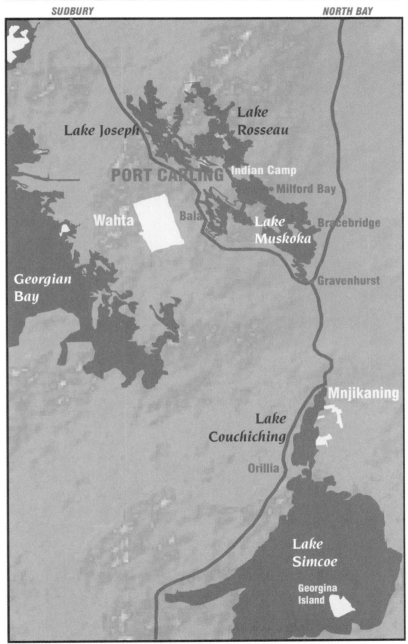

SUDBURY

NORTH BAY

Lake Joseph

Lake Rosseau

PORT CARLING

Indian Camp

Milford Bay

Wahta

Bala

Lake Muskoka

Bracebridge

Georgian Bay

Gravenhurst

Mnjikaning

Lake Couchiching

Orillia

Lake Simcoe

Georgina Island

TORONTO

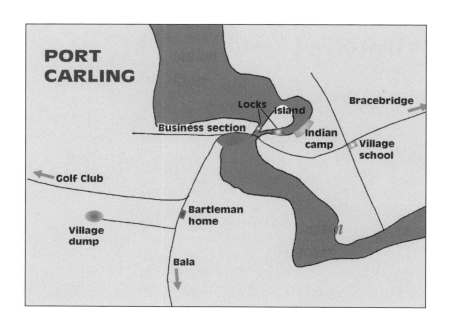

Foreword

I FIRST BECAME AWARE of the Hon. James K. Bartleman, Ontario's 27th Lieutenant Governor, in 1998 when he was nominated for the National Aboriginal Achievement Award, an awards system recognizing career achievement operated by and for the Canadian Aboriginal community.

As I read Jim's nomination, I felt great pride in knowing that an Aboriginal from northern Ontario had risen through the ranks of Canada's foreign service to become one of Canada's most senior diplomats. Since so few Aboriginal people attain such success in Canada, it occurs to me that Jim's life story must be an interesting study in humanity.

Jim received the National Aboriginal Achievement Award in 1999 and was honoured in a gala ceremony before a national audience of Aboriginal, corporate, and government leaders which subsequently aired as a CBC television special. The award represents the highest honour that the Aboriginal community bestows upon its own achievers.

As the producer and writer of Jim's video biography for the CBC program, I had the pleasure of meeting Jim and learning about his life. I found that we shared many similarities. Jim's parents were friends of my Mohawk grandparents who spent the summers in Port Carling where Jim grew up. We each had one Aboriginal parent and one non-Aboriginal parent. Like many other Aboriginal people of mixed heritage, we had spent a great deal of our youth in search of our identity and trying to reconcile both sides of our heritage. As Aboriginal men, we both selected non-traditional careers working in the service of the betterment of others and in the interest of our country.

Having worked with some of the world's most colourful political leaders, Jim has distinguished himself by successive appointments to more senior diplomatic posts—including Cuba, Israel, NATO, and South Africa—in a career that has spanned 35 years.

Jim's journey also illustrates the promise of Canada as a tolerant nation where diversity can be respected and accepted and that a boy of limited means born on the wrong side of the tracks can overcome racial discrimination and poverty to rise through the ranks of Canadian society to eventually sit with and advise the Prime Minister of Canada.

Jim's keen interest in history and political events provides an insight to the evolution of northern Ontario and underscores Jim's personal accounts and feelings regarding the social conditions of Aboriginal people of the last several generations.

I feel a sense of pride in knowing Jim. He is greatly admired and a real mentor for Aboriginal people and other Canadians alike. He has persevered to overcome obstacles and is the author of a life well-lived. In reading this book, I sense that Jim has finally reconciled both sides of his ancestry and is at peace with himself and the world.

I am honoured to be Jim's friend, a son of Canada, an elegant diplomat, a caring father and family man, an Aboriginal leader in his own right, and the Queen's representative for the good people of Ontario.

— *John Kim Bell*, Founder & President, National Aboriginal Achievement Foundation

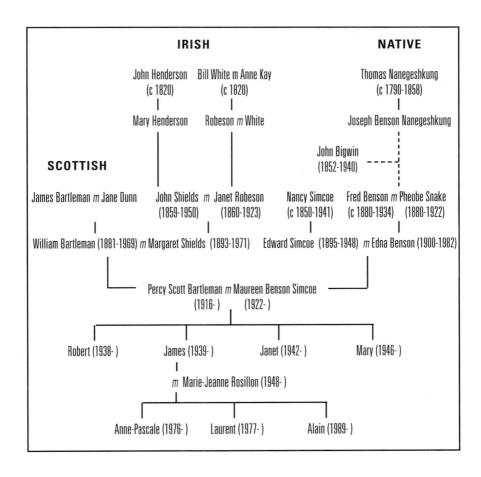

IRISH   NATIVE

John Henderson   Bill White m Anne Kay   Thomas Nanegeshkung
    (c 1820)   (c 1820)   (c 1790-1858)

Mary Henderson   Robeson m White   Joseph Benson Nanegeshkung

                                          John Bigwin
SCOTTISH   (1852-1940)

James Bartleman m Jane Dunn   John Shields m Janet Robeson   Nancy Simcoe   Fred Benson m Pheobe Snake
                                (1859-1950)   (1860-1923)   (c 1850-1941)   (c 1880-1934)   (1880-1922)

William Bartleman (1881-1969) m Margaret Shields (1893-1971)   Edward Simcoe (1895-1948) m Edna Benson (1900-1982)

              Percy Scott Bartleman m Maureen Benson Simcoe
                    (1916-)   (1922-)

Robert (1938-)   James (1939-)   Janet (1942-)   Mary (1946-)

            m Marie-Jeanne Rosillon (1948-)

Anne-Pascale (1976-)   Laurent (1977-)   Alain (1989-)

The author, with his wife Marie-Jeanne, meets Nelson Mandela upon taking up the post as Canada's high commissioner to South Africa in 1998.

Prologue

Canada's envoy to South Africa was shocked with a cattle prod, beaten to a pulp, tied up and robbed in his Cape Town hotel room late Thursday night. High Commissioner James Bartleman 59, who had come to Cape Town from his base in Pretoria to attend South African President Nelson Mandela's last speech to legislature before his retirement, had just checked in to his room when he was attacked.
— *Ottawa Citizen*, February 6, 1999

1

It was a violent mugging, no different from the dozens that occurred daily during the ongoing crime wave infecting South Africa in February 1999. This time I was the victim.

The Canadian government had named me high commissioner to the post-apartheid country of Nelson Mandela in August 1998. A 33-year veteran of the foreign service, I had requested the posting after more than four years as Prime Minister Chrétien's diplomatic advisor. My wife, Marie-Jeanne, whom I had met and married twenty-four years earlier during a posting to NATO headquarters in Brussels, was born in the former Belgian Congo and wanted to live in Africa again. I had served in Latin America, Europe, Asia, and the Middle East, and wanted to round off my career in Africa, which had always held a fascination for me.

Life could not have been rosier—or so it seemed. On a personal level, my family was close and supportive. Our two older children were doing well academically: Anne-Pascale, 23, was enrolled in a doctoral program in health sciences at the University of Guelph; Laurent, 22, was at the University of Saskatchewan Law School; and Alain, our gift of later life, was a bright, affectionate nine-year-old, happily attending the American International School in Johannesburg. My parents, unlike those of most of my friends of a similar age, were alive, healthy, and proud of the achievements of their son.

Professionally, I had been entrusted with progressively more senior responsibilities over the course of a long diplomatic career, holding ambassadorial appointments to Cuba, to Israel, and to the North Atlantic Council at NATO headquarters in Brussels. On the home front, I basked in the esteem of the people of the small Ontario village of Port Carling in the district of Muskoka, where I had spent my boyhood and youth, and I had just been nominated to receive a prize for lifetime achievement in public service from one of the major Canadian Aboriginal organizations.

Back to the scene of the crime. South Africa has three capital cities: Pretoria (administrative) in the north; Bloemfontein (justice) in the centre; and Cape Town (legislative) on the South Atlantic. Canada maintained homes or official residences for its high commissioner at Pretoria and Cape Town. My predecessors, who had not been accompanied by children, spent six months of the year in Cape Town, when Parliament was in session, and the other six months in Pretoria, where the bulk of South Africa's public servants were located. Marie-Jeanne and I decided soon after our arrival to mothball the residence in Cape Town and to live year-round in Pretoria in order to provide a stable home life for Alain. I would cover Parliament by flying periodically to Cape Town, where I would lodge in a hotel.

On the day of the mugging I had been in Pretoria, hosting a meeting of Canadian ambassadors and high commissioners from neighbouring diplomatic missions in sub-Saharan Africa. Assistant Deputy Minister Joseph Caron, responsible for African relations in the Department of Foreign Affairs, had flown in for the occasion. As is usual in gatherings of this sort, we exchanged views on how to promote Canada's interests in the countries of our accreditation, noting how difficult this had become in view of the decline in living standards and life expectancies, the rise in HIV-AIDS infection rates, the growth of corruption, and the spread of warfare and banditry. All of us were dedicated to finding ways of reorienting Canada's policies toward this part of the world, by helping peoples neglected by the forces of globalization. We hammered out a series of proposals for Joseph to take back for consideration in Canada. I then said goodbye to my guests and caught an early evening flight to Cape Town, some 1,300 kilometres away. The next day President Mandela was scheduled to make his last speech to Parliament before his retirement; I was to represent Canada.

During the two-hour flight I glanced distractedly at the daily newspapers. They were what the British would call "broadsheets": serious publications, similar to *The Globe and Mail* or the *National Post*, that did not as a matter of course feature crime and sex scandals to attract a readership. Nevertheless, with more than 26,000 murders occurring each year and with a rape taking place on average every four minutes, crime was the national preoccupation, and even the serious press had to cover the most blatant cases of the day.

A senior South Korean business executive, I noted, had been murdered during a botched robbery in Johannesburg; not wanting any witnesses to their holdup, thieves had locked six meat workers in the back of their truck in Soweto, leaving them to die in the airtight compartment surrounded by chilled sides of beef; and criminals in Cape Town, after cleaning out the cash register, had drowned the owner of a small pizzeria by submerging his head in a pail of water.

I paid little attention. The thought crossed my mind that the last minutes of the meat workers must have been terrible; according to the press reports, the workers, seeking to free themselves as the air ran out, clawed at the door before collapsing and dying. The fate of the pizzeria proprietor made me think of the death scene in *The Name of the Rose*, where a monk is murdered by immersion in a vat of liquid pig fat. Death by suffocation, I thought, must be the worst way to go.

A driver whisked me from the airport to the Winchester Mansions hotel, on the seafront at the foot of the Cape Mountains. I didn't know the place, but the Canadian consulate in Cape Town had made the reservations, assuring my secretary in Pretoria that it was clean, comfortable, and safe. Other members of my staff had stayed there and had been happy enough with the quality of the accommodations. There seemed to be no reason to doubt the brochure put out by the hotel, which said that the Winchester Mansions embodied "the style and gracious hospitality of a bygone era" and recalled "a more genteel age, when courtesy and personal attention were paramount."

The personal attention I received was of a different nature.

Fifteen minutes after checking in, I was fighting for my life. A black, neatly dressed, heavily built individual in his early thirties had come to the door to say that the front desk had asked him to check the condition of the fan. When I turned my head to see if in fact there was a problem, my visitor pressed an electric stun gun against my stomach, pulled the trigger, and released 50,000 volts of electricity into my body.

I did not collapse, as I should have done after absorbing such a massive charge, but fought back. Shouting "No! No! No!" I stepped back to kick him as hard as I could. The thought occurred to me that brave men probably remain silent as they fight off interlopers, but I continued yelling just the same. I looked into the man's eyes. They were blank, impersonal, and hostile. I meant nothing to him as a person. I was an Aboriginal Canadian, but to him I was just one more rich white man, of the same race and social status as the South African European elite that had oppressed blacks, coloureds, and Asians for generations under apartheid. I was probably not even the first person he had mugged.

My hair tingled from the shock of the electricity. My mind wandered, bringing into focus an image from a science fair I had visited some years earlier, when smiling children put their hands on an electric ring and squealed with delight as the static electricity made their hair stand on end. I saw, as if from afar, that I had knocked my assailant to the floor, but he was rising to his feet, the look in his eyes no longer neutral, but angry and determined. My foot was broken and out of commission. Without thinking, I drove my fist into his face. Overpowering pain engulfed my hand. It was as if I had hit a piece of concrete. At the age of 59, I was too old for this kind of nonsense.

He didn't even blink, but smashed his fist against my

jaw, cutting my mouth and jarring my teeth. None broke. Perversely, I made a mental note to compliment my dentist in Pretoria for the quality of his recent bridgework. As I backed away, throwing ineffectual punches, I listened to myself screaming, as if the cries were coming from someone else. He then delivered a blow that broke my nose and precipitated a cascade of blood over my body, onto him, and over the rug and the bedroom furniture.

I no longer wanted to fight. My assailant, however, was just beginning. After giving me a thorough beating, he stopped to say that if I did not co-operate and shut up he would kill me. He had a gun, he said, and would use it if need be.

"Take what you want and get out," was my answer. He was in no hurry, preferring to bind my hands behind my back with my neckties and search my briefcase and luggage at leisure. All he could find was 1,200 rand (about 300 dollars). He became even nastier, slapping me around and demanding to know where I had hidden the money. He had seen me arrive by chauffeur-driven limousine, dressed in an expensive suit. Obviously I was a rich man. He didn't understand my explanation that as a diplomat I received a clothing allowance for representation purposes, but in reality was just a moderately paid public servant.

As I talked to him, I looked over his shoulder at the television; an obscure piece of South African drama was being enacted. The actors strutted across the stage, oblivious to my distress and leaving me with the feeling that I too was just playing a part in a play, and that what was happening to me wasn't real. My world began to dissolve.

Like everyone else, I had my routine. I rose in the morning

and went to bed at night. In between, I ate, drank, read the newspaper, went to work, argued, consoled, gossiped, played games with my son, listened to music, watched television, and revelled in the company of a close and loving family, complete with a faithful dog we had brought from Canada. I had, however, been struggling with a depression that had been growing in intensity over the previous three years. Moreover, sometimes at night I had a nightmare: I dreamt that I was a poor half-breed kid in the small Ontario village of Port Carling dreaming that he had become a diplomat who had successfully faced challenge after challenge to rise to the top of his profession. I would then awake (still within the dream) to find myself back in Muskoka, the half-breed kid once again afraid to leave the village and confront the outside world.

This dream or a variant of it had been visiting me periodically for more than three decades. I would wake up uneasily, the dream within the dream fresh; but the memory of it would fade and I would get on with life. Every so often, however, no matter what I was doing or where I was, the memory would reappear. I would wonder whether I was inside or outside my dream. This would lead me to ask myself two questions: Who am I anyway? Have I earned the right to such success as I have had?

My captor paced back and forth, talking on his cellular tele-phone to an accomplice elsewhere in the building or outside in the street; he was reluctant to leave with such a paltry haul after having taken the risk of penetrating one of Cape Town's better hotels. Every few minutes he returned to cuff me on the head, demanding, as in a grade-B movie, that I tell him where the money was hidden. At last he decided to leave. He pushed me forward on the bed and started to force a piece of underclothing down my throat; he wanted to be sure I wouldn't raise the alarm as he made his getaway.

In the course of my career in the foreign service, I have been held up by bandits in Latin America, hit by rocks during the Intifada in Israel, forced to make an emergency landing on board a military helicopter in northern Italy, and almost swept to my death in a raging river in Labrador while a guest of Canada's military. I had escaped disaster so often that I had come to think I was invulnerable.

This time it was different. I found myself engaged in a desperate attempt to remain alive. My broken nose was filled with congealing blood, and I couldn't breathe. I would die a horrible death by suffocation just like the people I had read about on the flight to Cape Town unless I could remove the gag. I managed to spit it out.

My persecutor was starting to stuff it back in when I began to beg for my life. I told him I would surely die if he forced the gag down my throat. I had a wife who would be widowed and children left without a father. I would make no noise as he made his departure. Why not simply tie me to an armchair? He could trust me.

He looked at me carefully, perhaps seeing for the first time that I was a human being. He resumed his pacing, waving the underclothing in a distracted manner as he decided my fate. I continued to seek to reach him on a personal level, telling him that the cashmere sports coat and Hermes tie that he had stolen from my wardrobe suited him and saying the Jaeger-LeCoultre watch (a wedding anniversary gift from my wife) went well with his new wardrobe.

Suddenly he stopped and approached me, saying he would let me live. Thrusting his face up to mine, he said that if I called out or provided the police with any details about what had happened, members of his gang in Pretoria (called, he said, the Gestapo) would kill my wife and family. He bound me to the armchair so tightly that the marks on my arms and legs took almost a month to disappear, and walked to the door. Then he turned around and came back. I thought he had changed his mind and it was the end.

Instead, he said, "I'm sorry," and left the room. I was devastated. This petty thief, after brutalizing, humiliating, and robbing me, was now seeking to deny me the right to hate him.

The next few days passed in a blur. Prime Minister Chrétien called immediately to express his shock and to provide comfort. Hundreds of colleagues sent messages of goodwill. Others started a rumour, still alive and reopening wounds years later, that I had been beaten up in a bar. The departmental press officer called to offer his best wishes and to remind me of the unwritten code all Canadian diplomats who are victims of crime or conflict when posted abroad must follow: play down the gravity of the incident to avoid offending the host government. I complied. The story became headline news in Canada but was quickly forgotten.

I was shaken to the core. The dream within a dream appeared each night with such intensity that soon I was afraid to go to bed. It was as if the grovelling I had had to do to survive had destroyed my sense of identity and resurrected old struggles over existential issues that I had come to terms with as a child and youth. Flashbacks, not of the mugging but of the dream within a dream, invaded my life. I was terrified that I would awake and find myself back in Port Carling in the late 1940s.

If I wanted to recover, I would have to address the questions raised by my dreams.

High Commission personnel had their own personal problems, and needed me more than I needed them. To make matters worse, other staff members—Canadian and South African, white and black—themselves became crime victims, including a driver who lost a leg after being shot gratuitously following a mugging in Soweto. I had faced and dealt with problems as difficult in previous postings as ambassador. This time I didn't have the will to cope. When the prime minister proposed we make a fresh start in Australia, Marie-Jeanne and I accepted the offer. First, though, I had to take myself in hand. But how? The answer, it seemed, lay in seeking professional help, and in responding to the message of my dream within a dream. I would relive my past to find peace in the present.

2

I wrote the following memoir in spare moments over the next two years, focussing on my boyhood and youth in the small central Ontario village of Port Carling, Muskoka, in the years immediately after the Second World War. At first I blamed problems of identity and early childhood poverty for creating a personality so fragile that it would collapse in the face of a mugging. I pulled myself together as I realized that the racial discrimination and poverty I had experienced were no different from what millions of Canadians endured at that time and continue to experience today. I, however, had been the lucky one. My family had emerged from poverty; iconic figures of rare power from both the Indian and white sides of my heritage had served as role models; my close idiosyncratic

family had provided emotional support and colour; a benefactor had sent me to university; I had travelled to Europe at
a time of great change in postwar history; and against the
odds I had become a diplomat and a representative of my
country.

The author's father, Percy Bartleman, seen here in the late 1930s, could have been a character out of a Mark Twain novel.

One
A Time Primeval

Dr. Stephen Leacock, noted Canadian author and Emeritus
Professor of Political Economy at McGill University, played a
prominent part in the rescue of Percy Bartleman of Orillia Ontario,
whose sailing canoe capsized on storm-tossed Lake Couchiching
on July 9.
   — *McGill News*, September 1939

1

The summer of 1946 was a time of innocence. The notions of
poverty, racial discrimination, social marginalization, alienation from God, and death meant nothing to me.

   One quiet Sunday afternoon in June, a taxi delivered
my mother, my brother, my two sisters, myself, rucksacks,
and an assortment of pots and pans to a tent near the dump
in the small Muskoka village of Port Carling, where I was to
spend my boyhood and youth. I was six, Bob was eight, Janet
was four, and Mary just two months. My father was white
and my mother Indian, a distinction we children never
noticed. Always having had a roof over our heads and plenty
to eat, we didn't know our family was dirt-poor and at the
bottom of the social scale. Never having attended church, we
were unaware that the Christian world was divided into the
saved and the damned. All of this would change when school
started in the fall.

   My father was waiting for us, a large welcoming smile

on his face. He had come to Port Carling a month earlier to visit his Indian father-in-law, who lived in the small Indian reserve known locally as the Indian Camp, and had decided to stay—at least for a while. His ambition was to go north to take up a homestead near the Ojibwa reserve of Shawanaga, on Georgian Bay, where my mother had relatives. In the interim, he had found work shovelling gravel and loading rock on trucks by hand for a local businessman for sixty cents an hour. Not being Indian, he wasn't allowed to remain with his father-in-law at the Indian Camp; he constructed a rough shelter from rusty pieces of corrugated iron at the village dump and saved his money until he could buy a tent and send for his family.

Our family had spent the war years in a tough, multi-ethnic area of Welland, Ontario, where my father was a steel worker. Our neighbours included Canadians of French, Hungarian, Jewish, Polish, and Italian origin; half-breed kids fitted easily into the mix. Everyone was working-class and described themselves as such. Literally on the other side of the tracks, the quarter was boxed in by railway spur lines. The sound of locomotives shunting boxcars was part of our life, as were the shouts and laughter of drunks on Saturday nights.

Bob and I revelled in this classless rough-and-tumble world. We regularly skipped school to play with our friends along the railway tracks. We engaged in petty vandalism, slipping into the sheds of neighbours to open cans of paint and splatter their contents on the walls or simply mix them together for malicious pleasure. At times, we stole toys left outside by other children. Our mother did her best to control us, but we didn't care; we were enjoying our undisciplined pursuits too much.

Our father likewise lived a free life to the full. He prepared enormous quantities of homemade raisin wine and invited his buddies over to drink. A natural storyteller, he held court in the living room, recounting the dramatic events of his life. Bob and I shared his pride in dropping out of school at the age of fourteen, and dodging the truant officer, who wanted to send him to the reformatory for delinquent boys. He would also describe his adventures as a hobo during the Great Depression, riding the rails across Canada, hiding from the railway police, knocking on doors to ask for food in exchange for doing chores, working as a lumberjack and farm labourer, and begging on street corners.

Inevitably, he would produce a well-worn newspaper clipping describing an incident some years earlier that had provided his fifteen minutes of fame. My white grandmother had obtained a job as cook, and one of my aunts as maid, for Stephen Leacock, whose summer home was in Orillia, my father's hometown. My father had taken his canoe out on Lake Couchiching just as an enormous storm blew up. When my grandmother appealed to Leacock to save him, Canada's best-known humorist rode his motorboat to the rescue and hauled my father from the water against his will—my father claimed that he was in greater danger from being run over by Leacock's launch than from drowning. Leacock poured himself and my father, still a teenager, water glasses of whisky and telephoned *The Toronto Star* to ensure that the world knew that the author of *Sunshine Sketches of a Little Town* had rescued an Orillia boy. The story was picked up by the wire services and carried in the international press, including *The Times* of London.

My mother was the real head of the family, utterly devoted to her children. She did her best to keep my father's wild instincts under control, periodically taking a hammer and smashing the crock he fermented his wine in, as well as the gallon bottles he stored it in. My father was not to be discouraged; after my mother had calmed down, he would come home with a new supply of wine-making equipment and start again. Married at fourteen (she told the United Church minister she was eighteen), she had a hard life. My parents initially supported themselves by cutting firewood for a farmer in exchange for groceries and a rudimentary roof over their heads. They later teamed up with Indian relatives of my mother, living in tents on vacant land on the shores of Lake Muskoka, picking blueberries to sell to tourists on the side of the highway and fishing, peddling the catch to local restaurants.

My brother Bob was born at this time, with an older cousin of my mother from the reserve serving as midwife. A six-quart basket served as a bassinet, and milk purloined from a nearby cow provided Bob's first meal. The rest of us were born before my mother's twenty-second birthday, none of us in hospitals. An unskilled labourer, and a nomad at heart, my father then moved from job to job before ending up in Port Carling.

Port Carling's reputation in postwar Ontario as one of Canada's leading tourist centres meant nothing to me at the time. I had no idea that it constituted a microcosm[1] of what would become the globalized world of the twenty-first century, with its winners and its losers squeezed into one small village of no more than 500 permanent residents and several thousand summer residents, within a block of a few square kilometres. Nor did I suspect that it would have been difficult to find in Canada a place where the contrasts between rich and poor, sophisticated and rude, city and country, gentile and Jew, American and Canadian, and descendants of original settlers and newcomers were more pronounced. The Indians were the invisible brown minority at the bottom of the heap.

I only knew that an exciting summer was in store for the Bartleman children, living outdoors with our family in a tent on the side of the gravel road that wended its way over a large hill from the main street of the village to the village dump. There was also the prospect of spending time with my Indian grandfather, my Indian uncle, and various Indian great-uncles and great-aunts, who, as always, were spending the summer at Port Carling in their modern-day ghetto at the Indian Camp.

2

My father had erected the tent on the property of an aged former prospector named Pat Paddington, who had drifted to Port Carling with his Indian wife, Violet, and her adult daughter, Stella. Pat was eking out an existence as a casual labourer and had built a small cabin with a leaky tin roof that sounded like a drum when it rained. Pat and Violet were kind to the Bartleman brood. We spent long afternoons in their cabin drinking in the scent of sweetgrass and listening to my mother and her two Indian friends murmuring in Chippewa while they fashioned baskets from strips of white ash and transformed porcupine quills, beads, and birch bark into fancywork, the local term for handicraft. Stella had tuberculosis, like so many thousands of Indians at that time, and died shortly after we arrived in Port Carling.

We were proud of our large tent, and considered that

our location close to the village dump presented opportunities rather than disadvantages. Granted, the dump had its own distinctive fragrance, and the permanent black cloud of smoke from burning orange crates, cardboard, scrap lumber, and discarded furniture was not to everyone's taste. But where else could one find treasures such as slightly soiled but usable toys and somewhat torn but still readable comic books, and see wildlife (including raccoons and skunks) in profusion, not to mention flocks of seagulls and crows, which constantly circled over their culinary delights.

Fire from the burning garbage spread that summer into the bush, causing an enormous forest fire. We had first-row seats as the villagers fought it to a standstill in the meadow below the rocky outcrop on which our tent was located. Ferndale House, a large resort on Lake Rosseau two miles from the village, also went up in flames that summer. From our campsite high above the village, we heard the frantic pealing of church bells late one evening summoning the men of the village to assemble at the fire hall, and then, somewhat later, the sirens of the venerable fire truck as it hastened, followed by a convoy of firefighters and the curious, to the hopeless fight with the inferno. My father's employer was later engaged, with every other trucker in the area, to haul the debris to the dump. Fire-blackened cans of pineapples, pears, peaches, and a variety of vegetables and soups were dropped off at our tent. The labels on the cans burnt off, we children played a game guessing the contents before opening them. We were winners when the reward was fruit rather than vegetables.

The gravel road to the dump, which could have been taken from a scene in Erskine Caldwell's *Tobacco Road*, had its own history. Some years before, the village council had decided to expropriate land for the road from an irascible old-timer who vowed that he would die rather than allow a road to disgrace the land of his pioneer forebears. He blasted a giant ditch across the path to be taken by the work crews and erected a fence to stop intruders. When the village constable tried to remove the fence, he learned to his sorrow that it had been electrified. The old-timer was sent to jail for his antics but he was released unrepentant and, seeking to scandalize the good burghers of the village who had violated his property, deliberately slept off his drunken binges on the front lawn of the Canadian Legion. He accordingly won a village reputation as an anti-hero, admired by many for his nonconformist approach to civic duty. My mother, who had been the victim of his racist remarks when she was a little girl, had no time for this historical revisionism.

Pat Paddington had the pleasure of sharing the Dump Road with two other families. The neighbour at the base of the hill lived with his wife and daughter in an old log cabin, well known to my mother, who had often accompanied her father on visits to the household when she was a child. By the summer of 1946, however, the house was collapsing around its owners. The end was in sight when a stout lady who had had too much to drink started to dance a jig during a party and fell through the floor. Then the daughter was hit by a car and killed, demoralizing the family, who abandoned house and village to make a fresh start in Orillia.

This was my first encounter with death. My six-year-old companion and I had played among the weeds and the long grass in her backyard, our legs wet from morning dew and our bare feet sticky from stepping in the soft droppings of the free-ranging chickens. We had searched for eggs among the straw, almost overwhelmed by the pungent odour of ammonia in the airless chicken coop. The next day she was dead, the first of three village children who would die violent deaths from accidents in my Port Carling years.

I would see much death in my foreign service career: corpses lying among the crowds on the sidewalks of Dacca; Mother Teresa carried in great pomp and dignity on an open bier at her funeral in Calcutta; a Russian drug lord, victim of a gangland killing, powdered and laid out in ostentatious splendour in an Orthodox church in Moscow; a beautiful Israeli woman being lowered without a coffin into a grave among the orange groves of the Judean hills; and the mummified bodies of Lenin and Ho Chi Minh in their mausoleums in Moscow and Hanoi. They would all look like my dead schoolmates in their open coffins at the village churches from my Muskoka youth—merely sleeping.

3

The other neighbour, an ancient villager who looked as though he had arrived with the first pioneers but had forgotten to die, had the privilege of sharing the top of the hill with Pat Paddington, and lived in an unpainted shack with a pigsty and an outhouse in the backyard, each competing to emit the worse odour. The master of the house spent his days sitting in a rocking chair, corncob pipe clamped between the blackened stumps of his few remaining teeth, watching loads of garbage go by. From time to time he would venture to the dump to collect a supply of rotting fruits and vegetables for his pig before resuming his inactivity. A granddaughter lived with him, but refused to speak to the Bartleman children. We were too far down the social ladder for her taste.

Social position was the last thing on my mind that summer of 1946. I recall the burning heat of the day and the incessant chirping of crickets in the evenings, a setting I was to be reminded of many years later when travelling in southern France, near the Mediterranean. My brother Bob and I (our sisters being too young to join in) kept ourselves busy with cow-dung fights, using dry manure collected in a nearby pasture as ammunition. We gathered wild strawberries among the weeds and grass near a fenced-off water hole, which always smelled fresh and humid, even on the hottest days.

I was the berry-picker of the family, disappearing into the bushes on the side of the dusty road to collect baskets of raspberries in July and blackberries in August, seeking out a spot where I could sit undisturbed for hours among the brambles to watch birds, insects, and the clouds in the Muskoka sky. I would return to the tent, hands and mouth red from juice, legs and arms scratched from thorns, looking forward to praise from my mother for a job well done.

Mother, Mary, the author, Janet, and Bob go swimming in the Indian
River in 1947.

Two
Reality

Race is like a car left with its engine running. The slightest touch will put it in gear and set it speeding towards some bitter accident.
— Graham Spry, "One Nation, Two Cultures,"
The Canadian Nation

1

Nirvana ended with the summer. My education in the social and racial realities of Muskoka village life began when my father decided to spend the winter in the village.

    Living in a tent near the village dump admittedly provided neither the best address nor the most auspicious way to start a new life, and he sought desperately to find permanent accommodation for his family. No one was interested in renting to an unconventional, poorly paid, highly opinionated labourer, new to the village, who would tell anyone who would listen that he intended to move north at the earliest opportunity to take up a homestead. A woman who agreed to take us changed her mind at the last minute. A neighbouring resort owner then materialized to offer my father an uninsulated two-bedroom summer cottage on the Indian River. It came with cracks in the outer walls, defective electrical wiring fashioned from discarded telephone cables, and an outside toilet. My father had to agree to purchase all his firewood from the owner and vacate the premises before the first tourist arrived in May of the following year.

The woman who had accepted and then rejected the Bartlemans as tenants was furious when she learned that her fellow tourist lodge owner had rented one of his cottages to us. She told my father that the individual who had taken us in, at avaricious rates, had in fact earlier tried to dissuade her from renting to us, saying that Percy Bartleman was really a gypsy, that his wife was Indian and not to be trusted, and that nothing could be worse than to have bedbug-ridden gypsy half-breed children on one's premises.

Our first year in Port Carling was hard; we were different, and treated as strangers. Our parents were closest to the Indians at the Indian Camp, but only a handful of them remained in the fall; the others did not return until the spring. One who did stay was Sam Williams, whose daughter, hospitalized with tuberculosis at the time in the government sanitarium at Gravenhurst, had been my mother's closest friend as a youngster. Sam radiated a sense of inner peace, impressing me enormously with his innate wisdom. He and my Indian grandfather, who was similar in outlook, were to serve as role models. I was well aware, even at that early age, that if one's lot in life was likely to be poverty and toil, as mine was, then it was important to value peace of mind and wisdom in order to cope. Sam, unaware of my developing philosophy of life, gave me my first major material possessions: a .22-calibre rifle and an old rowboat.

The winter of 1946-1947 was bitterly cold. The sky was lit up at night by the northern lights and the stars, clouds of freezing mist hung over the river, and the snow crackled as we walked. After we went to bed, the fire in the wood stove would go out, a dusting of snow would penetrate the cracks in the walls, ice several centimetres thick would build up on the uninsulated windows, and a covering of frost would descend over everything, including the blankets on our beds. We three older children would make our way to our parents' bed to sleep with them and the baby to keep warm.

Each morning my father would rise early to light the fire. One day, out of kindling, he searched for dry branches along the banks of the river, which a strong current kept ice-free except along the shore. Spotting a dry branch, he ventured out on the ice, but broke through. Despite the minus-35-degree temperature, he pushed on to seize the branch, realizing that the only way to avoid death from hypothermia was to start a fire as soon as possible. His clothes quickly froze and icicles formed on his hair and eyebrows as he returned to the cottage. My mother then took over, lighting a fire and giving him dry clothing. He went to work that morning as if nothing unusual had happened.

During the winter my mother asserted herself, taking the family's future in her hands, perhaps sensing that my father was simply too romantic and impractical to make major domestic decisions. She sought better accommodation, paying no heed to my father's plans to move on in the spring to take up a homestead. She fixed her attention on a two-storey shack, with one room downstairs and two bedrooms upstairs, on a large lot with many apple trees on the side of a hill on the main street. Abandoned for years, the house had been occupied in the 1920s by a poverty-stricken family with some black in their heritage. The neighbours had shunned them even though they had been long-standing residents. The family had moved to a nearby town, where they prospered, but as a result of their treatment in Port Carling they refused to sell to their former neighbours, who wanted to tear down what had become known locally as the haunted house.

My mother went to see the owners and told them she could offer only a small down payment, but would sign over her family allowance cheques[2] to cover the balance. Remembering their own difficult days, they agreed to sell for 275 dollars, and we moved into our own house in the spring of 1947. The house was unpainted, the windows were broken, a water pipe protruded from a hole in the floor in one corner, the sawdust insulation that had been packed into the walls in the 1890s had long since disappeared, there was no electricity, and the floors slanted at a perilous angle. But it was home.

We took possession in May 1947, to the satisfaction of our landlord, who was able to rent our winter dwelling to better-paying tenants for the summer season. My parents thoroughly cleaned our new home, throwing out newspapers and broken pieces of furniture that had lain undisturbed for twenty years. A portion of a natural history encyclopaedia that we found remained one of my prized possessions for years. They whitewashed the walls and ceilings before moving in our worldly possessions, delivered to the front door by my father's trucker employer.

My father installed a wood stove purchased by mail order from Simpsons department store in Toronto; with the help of my mother, he strung stovepipes horizontally across the downstairs room (which served as living room, kitchen, dining room, and clothes closet) to an opening in an old brick chimney. The theory was that heat from the stove would pass through the stovepipes to warm the room. As far as I could tell, however, this elaborate arrangement simply made it difficult to keep the fire going and rendered the periodic cleaning of soot and creosote from the pipes that much more difficult and dirty.

My brother was given the job of lighting the fire each morning, but was soon relieved of his duty when my parents discovered that he was tearing boards off the back of the house for firewood. Fearing that the house might gradually disappear, like the Cheshire cat in *Alice's Adventures in Wonderland*, they thrust me into his place. From the age of eight until I left home at the age of seventeen, it was my responsibility to prepare dry kindling for my father to light fires, to help him cut wood in the bush and haul it home by sleigh with the aid of our malamute huskies, and to ensure that the family woodbox was always kept full. I loved my wood-cutting duties, welcoming the chance to spend time alone outdoors every evening, away from the hothouse atmosphere of the one room that confined the six Bartlemans and their household pets.

Our house, the only one in the village lacking electricity, was lit by kerosene lamps. We derived quiet, ignoble satisfaction whenever the power failed and our neighbours, scrambling to find lanterns and candles, found themselves reduced to our level. Toilet facilities consisted of an outdoor privy constructed out of three doors nailed together, with an often-missing fourth door for an entrance, located in a grove of sumach trees some fifty feet behind the house. We children considered it hilarious to see visitors try all four doors before gaining entrance to the odorous inner sanctum. An old copy of Eaton's catalogue, which in later years my brother Bob dubbed the Poor Boy's Playboy Magazine, provided paper. Visits to the outhouse were less entertaining in the winter, when we had to struggle through snow up to our bums (the path was never shovelled). We never lingered, given that we would usually find ourselves sitting, as if in Dogpatch in the comic strip, amid snow blown in through the open door.

Saturday nights were reserved for baths and for listening to the Toronto Maple Leafs take on all comers on "Hockey Night in Canada," broadcast from coast to coast on CBC radio. My mother would place a large tin washtub on the floor in the centre of the room and fill it with hot water from the kettle, kept boiling on the stove beside the bubbling soup pot filled with barley and beef bones, our main source of nourishing meals. We children would then be forced into the water one after the other, starting with Mary, the baby of the family. Bob, as oldest, was last, and he would always struggle to avoid the soapy water; my mother would usually have to take him by the ear and lead him to his fate amid much lamentation and tears. In the summers, with the advent of the swimming season, weekly baths were forgotten.

The house was intensely cold in the winter; the wood stove, in that era before air-tight stoves, would always go out during the night. After electricity was installed, we were able to put vegetables and milk into the refrigerator, which, when the temperature in the house fell below freezing point, would keep the cold out rather than in. To prevent the water pipes from freezing, the last person going to bed was supposed to ensure that the tap was left dripping. Inevitably someone would forget, and a desperate effort to thaw the pipes would begin, and often not finish for many hours.

These would be the occasions of real family dramas, rivalled for sheer domestic bad temper only by those associated with the ritual of stovepipe cleaning. In the absence of a trap door to the area under the floor where the water pipes were located, my father would be forced to clear the snow from an outside entrance so small that he would have to squeeze in on hands and knees. Once inside, he would crawl through dust and dirt impregnated with the droppings of the generations of cats and rodents who had adopted our house in its abandoned state in the years before we acquired it. In the dark, constricted space, my father would be obliged to push a flashlight and a kettle of boiling water ahead of him as he crept forward to search out frozen places on the galvanized steel pipe.

He would run out of hot water and call for more. With the pipes frozen, my mother would collect snow to dump into a large washtub on the stove, where it would melt and boil. Since the operation was time consuming, the thawed sections of the pipes would freeze again, leading to further recriminations. Occasionally my father would become so frustrated he would fashion a torch out of birchbark or old newspapers and apply the naked flame to the pipes, a highly dangerous operation, since one wayward spark could have set our tinder-dry house aflame.

One night, the family was aroused by the frantic barking of my pet terrier dog. I woke up in the bed that I shared with Bob on the upstairs hallway to the acrid smell of wet smouldering paper. My father was already on his way, rushing outside in the minus-30-degree weather in his long underwear, a fashion accoutrement of all Muskoka families in those days, to open the entrance to the space under the house. A torch of old newspapers he had used to thaw the pipes earlier in the day and that he thought he had snuffed out had come to life. My father extinguished the fire and returned to bed thoroughly shaken at the near tragedy.

Today, my encounters with outdoor toilets, kerosene-lamp lighting and wood-stove heating are confined to vacation trips in Canada's North. Marie-Jeanne and I, together with our children, have occupied six ambassadorial residences placed at our disposal to live in and to use for representational purposes over the past 25 years. More often than not, the elegant façades seen by the public and guests masked rot behind the scenes. In Havana, the residence roof was in such bad shape that we had to place 50-litre garbage pails at strategic locations to collect the water that poured through holes in the roof during the frequent tropical storms. I successfully appealed to President Castro for help after encountering difficulties in obtaining a local labour brigade to repair the residence, which resembled a 19th-century mansion from *Gone with the Wind* after the Union army had marched through Georgia. In Israel, the residence was a house set in an immense but weed-infested garden. We slept nervously at night aware that the attic over heads was a favourite nesting place for large venomous snakes. In South Africa, despite its location in an elegant neighbourhood and on a ridge overlooking Pretoria, the residence resembled a jail from the inside. Marie-Jeanne and I were both warders and prisoners. Every evening, we pulled heavy steel grills over every window and door and locked them firmly. Panic buttons, which could summon private heavily armed security guards, were located in every room. After thieves gained entrance to a neighbour's house robbing and raping the 66-year-old matron, we took our warder responsibilities with the utmost seriousness.

My family and I have enjoyed the comforts of these homes and revelled in their peculiarities. None, however, can match the hold our old house in Port Carling has maintained on me over the years. I can still picture every nook and cranny, see the crawl space under the stairs where my father kept his home-brew and where I stored my growing collection of books, smell the old unpainted lumber, experience the disorientation from walking over a floor six inches lower on one side of the room than on the other, and feel the cold from the heavily frosted single-pane windows in winter.

2

Introduction to school was not a happy experience. Bob and I were ill-prepared academically, and, to my bitter disappointment, I was forced to repeat a grade. I would spend twelve years receiving a solid, no-frills education at the four-room Port Carling Elementary and Continuation School, which closed its doors for good in the late 1950s. Two of my teachers were outstanding; two others, encountered from grades seven to ten, were brutal, browbeating the students for minor misdemeanours and enforcing discipline by frequent application of the strap upon hands and wrists. One of these would return to school after lunch in a bad mood after quarrelling with his wife and work off his rage on his students. His favourite tactic was to seize a yardstick and smash it down on his desk with a thunderous clap to make us properly fearful. He would then begin his rant, employing oratorical techniques that would have won the professional envy of a Fidel Castro. His first words in the deathly silent classroom would be almost inaudible, as he started to enumerate the various failings of his charges, who, he said, were indolent as well as of poor character; our grades, he would repeat, were disgraceful. The boys, he predicted, were destined to live the lives of ditchdiggers; the fate of the girls was to be even worse. His voice would rise as he listed our sins: not completing our homework assignments on time, talking during class, impertinence. His oration would come to a climax, if he was in good form, with a declaration delivered with all the hissing passion that he could muster: we were *so low that we couldn't slither under the belly of a snake!*

To compare his students to snakes was, to him, the worst form of condemnation and insult, since the serpent had tempted Adam and Eve and was, therefore, the most loathsome of beasts. Not surprisingly, he relished standing in whenever the mild-mannered Presbyterian minister responsible for providing religious instruction was absent. Clutching his well-worn Bible, he would stride up and down the aisles in full religious fury, venting his passion for his faith, his eyes flashing, daring the sinful to challenge him. I never did—although I wanted to.

Most of the boys left school as soon as they legally could, at age sixteen, unable or unwilling to master Latin and French (obligatory subjects in those days) and fed up with the petty tyranny of the teachers. Sometimes the departures were spectacular, with the student lunging at the teacher, the teacher beating the student with his fists, and the girls fleeing in tears, not to return until the next day, when classes would resume minus one expelled adolescent. I learned to keep my head down. My brother Bob wasn't as diplomatic; he left school as soon as he could.

3

In those early years, Bob and I had to endure racial taunts from older boys, who called us "dirty half-breeds." We had to fight a lot and did not always win. Bob, older and more recognizably Indian than I, had to bear the burden of the name-calling and bullying, but was never intimidated. One Saturday afternoon in the spring of 1947 we were set upon by a group of teenagers twice our size; they called my brother a "black bastard" and told both of us in a message laced with invective that Indians and half-breeds were unwelcome in the village and that the time was overdue for the Bartlemans to return from whence they had come, wherever that was.

Bob and I fought fire with fire, providing our opinion on the ancestry of their mothers before fleeing to what we thought would be the refuge of our home, the aroused bullies on our heels. To our surprise, the teenagers did not stop at the property line, but chased us up the path to our front door, which they kicked and yanked in an effort to get at us. We were dismayed to find that neither of our parents was at home. It looked as if we were in for a thorough beating, since the flimsy screen door, fastened only with a lightweight lock, would not resist for long.

I cowered in one corner of the room, but Bob did not hesitate; he grabbed the rifle Sam Williams had given me, loaded it in front of our attackers, and pulled back the hammer as he thrust the barrel into their astonished faces. He would have fired had our tormentors managed to open the door, and they knew it. They backed away, calling Bob a "crazy Indian" and vowing to exact their revenge in the schoolyard.

Another time I was chopping a fishing hole in the ice when a child from a nearby house came out to repeat in a mindless refrain, "Half-breed! Half-breed! Dirty half-breed!" The next thing I knew I was at his front door, having chased him in a blind rage, axe in hand, all the way to his home.

Even my mother was not spared. Late one afternoon she was waiting on the veranda as usual when Bob and I returned home from school. Suddenly a large raw-boned kid about sixteen years old started braying from the sidewalk,

"Filthy Squaw! Filthy Squaw! Go back to your filthy reserve! You're not wanted here!" I could see how hurt my mother was but she said nothing either to us or to my father. She wanted desperately to fit in to village life and was afraid of causing trouble. Within the year, she paid the price for her exposure to racism, for the abuse she had sustained as a child at home on the reserve, and for her desperate struggle to make ends meet on the wages of an unskilled labourer, by suffering a severe nervous breakdown, the consequences of which she would endure the rest of her life. She sought refuge in her children, determined that we would not lack the love she had been deprived of as a child; we reciprocated with the fierce protective instinct of the very young.

4

The death of the little girl on the Dump Road was followed by others of equal violence from accidents or suicides, making our introduction to community life resemble the beginning of a horror show. Matters started badly when I almost drowned.

Bob and I had joined a group of village children playing on a beach under the scorching August sun; he could swim but I could not. Two young teenagers lounged on the grass. One, the daughter of a cottager, spent her time applying lotion to her already well-tanned body, squinting into the sun and adjusting her sunglasses as she sought to deepen the golden brown of her face. The other, the strong-willed, red-haired daughter of a local farmer, her white skin betraying her days spent indoors helping her mother with household chores, kept up a steady banter with her younger brothers and sisters who were running along a dock to jump off the end. Bob and I joined in. I felt the burning heat of the planks on the soles of my feet as I followed my brother down the old wooden dock. I was looking forward to splashing in the cold water, which I assumed was only waist high.

I leapt, felt the shock of ice-cold water, and continued my downward plunge to touch no bottom. Bob was swimming back to shore unaware that I was drowning. I gasped for air and tried to call out only to swallow water and choke. I kicked my feet and tried to rise to the surface by thrashing around with my arms but continued to sink as if enveloped in a heavy viscous shroud. Suddenly, I was being hauled shoreward by my hair. The red-haired girl had come to the rescue. The others crowded around as she pounded water from my lungs and then returned to swimming when I began to suck in air. I sat shaking, suddenly clammy cold in the hot sun, listening distractedly as the summer visitor explained to no one in particular that she would have tried to help but her watch was not waterproofed and would have been ruined had she entered the water.

Death to villagers and cottagers alike from accidental drowning, trucks fully loaded with sand or building materials plunging through ice roads on the lakes, car crashes on deserted roads, or hunting misadventures—all these were part of the fabric of local life. And this does not include the heavy toll of cottagers and tourists drowned in those days before the introduction of strict water safety regulations. Suicide, it seemed, was the death of choice, with prominent villagers doing themselves in by drowning, carbon monoxide poisoning, and self-inflicted gunshot wounds. Usually we children would learn of suicides from death notices framed in black, taped to the front door of the general store and prominently displayed on the wall of the post office. These notices always sent a chill down my spine. All activity in the normally boisterous schoolyard would halt as the cortèges passed by on the way to one of the three churches, from which flowed the mournful pealing of bells before and after the funeral services. I once confessed my childish fears to someone who lived close to the cemetery, saying that in my imagination the dead came back to life after burial only to find themselves entombed under six feet of dirt. He obviously had thought about the matter; he told me in a lugubrious voice that I need not fear the dead, only the living. He committed suicide within the week.

Our house had its own macabre history. Soon after we moved in, our parents told us that several years earlier the next-door neighbour had hanged himself on an apple tree in what was to be our new backyard. My father helpfully added that the branch to which the rope had been attached had twisted so far out of shape that the departed, had he so wished, could have stretched out his feet and touched the ground. Bob and I dealt with our unease with black humour, saying that it was thoughtful of our neighbour to have lowered the branch; it allowed us to pick the sweetest apples on the tree without having to resort to a ladder.

However, the situation became worse, making even macabre joking inappropriate. Within months of our arrival, the neighbour on the other side of our house died in a hunting accident. It was the fall of 1948. My mother, like every other villager, quickly learned of the death, and asked the widow what she could do to help. She was told that the best service would be for me to keep the youngest child busy while the family tried to cope, so I was sent out to play with the son, who was only one year younger than myself. Neither one of us knew that his father was dead, and we watched with curiosity as the steady flow of village ladies arrived with offerings of home-baked goods to comfort the family. We both guessed that something momentous was happening, and suspected from the grim looks on the faces of visitors that the news, when we would eventually learn it, would not be good.

The family, bereft of a breadwinner, plunged into the deepest poverty. My companion, devastated by the death of his father, rebelled against the injustice of it all by walking out into the busy traffic and lying down on the road, daring drivers to run him over. He also stole from tourist cottages and, while still a child, was sent to a reformatory for delinquent boys. He once escaped and made it home to his family. A posse of heavily armed villagers swept down to search for him in our backyard. It was a black moonless night, and from within our house I heard the voices of the villagers, as excited as if they were hunting some dangerous wild animal rather than a frightened child, as they tramped through our rhubarb patch and searched our outdoor privy for my friend. My father chased them away, threatening to set our dogs on them if they did not get off our land. I will never forget my friend's screams of distress when they caught him, calling for his mother as the police pushed him into the back of a cruiser, its red rooftop light flashing, to return him to reform school, initiating a cycle of incarceration from which he would not emerge alive.

The intensity of this early exposure to suicide has meant that throughout my life I have wondered how it was possible for people to take their own lives. What drove people, whether young marginalized Natives or middle-class white villagers, to kill themselves? The explanations of Albert Camus, the

French existentialist author, that suicide was the central philosophical issue that all people had to address sooner or later
lacked credibility. Neither could I accept the musings of
Arthur Koestler, author of *Darkness at Noon*, who declared
that, psychologically, it was only natural to do oneself in
when life became unbearable. I paid more attention when
Ernest Hemingway shot himself, noting that his father had
done the same; I wondered if the father's behaviour had
influenced the son.

My attitude to suicide changed dramatically after I
was mugged. No longer was it a question for philosophical or
psychological musing. I fell into a deep post-traumatic
depression. A weight, heavier and more penetrating than anything purely physiological, pressed down on my chest,
destroying my will to live. I told Marie-Jeanne to throw my
ashes into the Indian River during the spring run-off from the
dam below the Indian Camp at Port Carling. In my mind,
dying would obviate the need for me to reconstruct my life,
and the mixing of my ashes with the water of this river, so
important to my Indian ancestors and to the early white pioneers, would reconcile the Indian and white natures of my
being and bring closure to my existence.

5

Even at an early age, I saw that poverty, hardship, and injustice were not a monopoly of Indians and half-breeds. The
local minister appeared on our doorstep on Christmas Eve
with a turkey with all the trimmings, which we politely
refused, suggesting that he take his gifts to a more needy
family. For there were white people worse off than the
Bartlemans. One was an old lady, the destitute daughter of

the first sawmill owner in the village, who lived with her fifty cats in one room of a house on the main street, scraping by on the revenue from the remainder of the building, which she rented to a local electrical contractor. Today she would be called a bag lady. She spent her time compulsively collecting old newspapers, magazines, and pieces of cardboard to add to the stacks of rubbish that clogged the corridors of her home. A familiar sight in the village, she shuffled along, bent over with age, always wearing the same dress and coat, a perpetual drop of moisture hanging from the end of her nose. I would often see her on a raft on the river after dark, furtively gathering driftwood.

Twenty years earlier, when she still had the money and the mental capacity, she had often invited young Indian girls from the Indian Camp home for hot lunches, a gesture of friendship my mother never forgot. My mother accordingly often asked her over for tea, and whenever the old lady was sick my mother insisted that she move in with us. My father ensured that she always had a good supply of firewood.

There was also an impoverished neighbour who constructed a modest house with an imposing outdoor toilet on a village road that led to a centre for Biblical studies. An elderly member of the family used to while away the hours sitting on his throne watching the well-heeled tourists pass by on their way to church, the door to the privy wide open, his underwear down around his ankles and his pipe in his mouth, providing a picture of pure Muskoka contentment for all to admire.

Eventually I became the paper boy charged with delivering this family's newspaper every evening, literally come rain, snow, or high water. The challenge was formidable. Their dog was well known in the village for following the family car to the general store whenever they went shopping, barking and attacking any human or dog that took its fancy, and it didn't like me. I would stand on the street shouting to the occupants to hold their vicious pet as I made a dash for the door. To make matters worse, the house was built on reclaimed swampland that flooded every spring; the husband, his face betraying the heart disease that would soon kill him, would stand silently at the open door of his one-room house, which was transformed into an island in the spring flood, holding his barking dog as I slopped through the water in my high rubber boots.

Late one black evening the wife came knocking on our front door. I can see her still, standing on the front porch, her face illuminated by the light from within our house, her grey hair blowing in the wind. "Perce," she said, "my husband's dead. Could you help me bury him?" My father, who had a generous nature but who was not at ease in situations like this, did not ask her in, but muttered that he would do what he could. Three days later my father and five of his friends, dressed in clean workclothes, carried the coffin to the grave. They were the only mourners other than family at the cemetery.

6

These were the bad years: poverty, racial discrimination, bullying, and gothic reality. The worst was over before I was ten, but the memory of exclusion remained with me for life, and was constantly rekindled through exposure to the Third World in my foreign service career. Everything, I was to discover with time, was relative. In Colombia in the mornings I had to step over abandoned street children, some as young as four, sleeping on the steps of the embassy covered only with newspapers in the cold of the high Andes mountains. In Bangladesh I saw naked mentally handicapped people, on hands and knees, foraging for food with dogs in the garbage. In Bosnia I saw a city whose occupants were living a hand-to-mouth existence in unheated, shell-shattered buildings. In South Africa I was stunned by the sight of shacks, housing millions of blacks living on less than one dollar a day, stretching off into the horizon in a country where swimming pools were the norm for the white minority.

Grandparents Edna and Ed Simcoe: Edna was brutal, but Ed was a role model for the author.

Three
Indian Roots

The Indian Village of Obogawanung, now Port Carling, consisted of some 20 log huts, beautifully situated on the Indian River and Silver Lake with a good deal of cleared land about it used as garden plots, and the Indians grew potatoes, Indian corn, and other vegetable products. They had no domestic animals but dogs and no boats but numerous birch bark canoes. The fall on the River there, being the outlet of Lake Rosseau, was about eight feet, and fish and game were very plentiful.
    — Vernon B. Wadsworth, *Reminiscences of Indians in Muskoka and Haliburton, 1860-1864*

1

Ontario today is not the Ontario of fifty years ago, but I still wonder how it was possible for a fair-minded and generous community to tolerate the hostility displayed by some of its members to the arrival of the Bartlemans. Was it because every group has its own social and economic hierarchy and newcomers should expect to struggle to be accepted? Was it because the local people, exposed to the lifestyles of summer visitors who maintained their own social, racial, and economic hierarchy, sought to emulate their betters by looking down on poor and racially different outsiders? Did our presence arouse a sense of unconscious collective guilt among the villagers? After all, white society in Canada as a whole had not yet started to deal with the way its ancestors had treated the Aboriginal people; could this guilt have been transformed into hostility toward anyone who reminded them of a past that did not conform to their image of their forebears as having been engaged in heroic efforts to tame and occupy a harsh land, which, in the prevailing myth, had been devoid of people? I came to the conclusion that these influences may have been at work, but the racism of the time was mainly responsible.

When the first white travellers to the future Port Carling arrived in the mid-nineteenth century, they were welcomed by the Indians of Obogawanung, the only permanent Indian settlement in the new District of Muskoka. According to Vernon Wadsworth, who visited the site as a member of a party of surveyors in 1860, theirs was a prosperous community of some twenty log cabins.[3] The government of the day ordered the removal of the people. The Indians petitioned the Crown to be allowed to remain:

"Father, this place is beautiful in our eyes and we found we could not leave it. Many winters have passed since we settled here and began to cultivate our gardens. We have good houses and large gardens where we raise much corn and potatoes....We live by hunting and taking furs....We hope you will grant the wish of your Red Children, and do it soon, because the whites are coming in close to us and we are afraid that your surveyors will soon lay out our lands here into lots."[4]

The request was denied. The Crown representative said that all lands in Muskoka had been surrendered in an 1850 treaty, and that the decision had already been taken to move them to a rocky, inhospitable reserve at Parry Island on Georgian Bay, near Parry Sound. By the end of the 1870s, the community was gone and the homes of the Native people were occupied by the first settlers. Only the small satellite reserve known as the Indian Camp, shared to this day by Chippewas and Mohawks, remained in the hands of the Indians.

Growing up, I often thought about what life had been like for the people of Obogawanung before the arrival of the white man, and their feelings when told they would have to abandon their homes. I often sensed their grieving spirits in the wind, the most powerful and lonely force I knew in my youth, whenever I walked alone near the river at night.

The end of Obogawanung did not spell the end of the Native presence in the soon-to-be-incorporated white village of Port Carling. Native families returned from their place of exile on Parry Island to trap and fish, and were joined in ever greater numbers by Chippewas from the Rama reserve, known today as the Mnjikaning First Nation, located to the south of Muskoka on the east side of the narrows between Lake Simcoe and Lake Couchiching.

These people, known in the nineteenth century as the Chippewas of the Lake Simcoe area,[5] had supported the British in the War of 1812 and the government side in the 1837 rebellion in Upper Canada. Nevertheless, they were removed from their farms, displaced from their community at the site of the future Orillia, and dispersed to the most marginal areas to be found anywhere in the region. The largest group was moved to Mnjikaning, onto lands that white pioneers had abandoned as being too rocky for cultivation; others from the same group were settled on reserves on Beausoleil Island and Christian Island on Georgian Bay, and on Snake Island on Lake Simcoe. Muskoka was their traditional hunting and fishing ground.

In the 1880s, in the wake of one of the periodic crises that affected them, Mohawks from the Oka reserve in Quebec (now known as the Kanesatake First Nation) were displaced to the newly created Gibson reserve (now known as the Wahta First Nation) in the backwoods of Muskoka near Bala. Traditional enemies of the Chippewas, they nevertheless joined them every summer in Port Carling to fish, trap, and sell fancywork to tourists. In the beginning, the Native peoples squatted on Crown land, erecting wigwams, tents, and tarpaper dwellings on the island between the dam and the locks. The government eventually set aside several acres of land exclusively for Native use, called it the Indian Camp, and administered it as part of the Mnjikaning and Wahta reserves.

Port Carling, therefore, was founded on the expulsion of a settled community in order to make way for another, of a different ethnicity and culture, which had more power. The establishment of the Indian Camp as the summer home for three groups of Native peoples, all of whom had been buffeted in the past by governments and settlers, was both a tribute to the resilience of the Indians and a belated gesture of fair play on the part of the government. This provided the basis for the creation of links of understanding between the two worlds—an opportunity that the people of that era did not think of exploiting.

2

My own links to the Native world were through my mother and my Indian grandparents, Edna Benson and Ed Simcoe,

Chippewa Indians with roots in the Lake Simcoe and Muskoka Lakes regions. My mother and her parents were members of the Mnjikaning reserve, but my mother lost her Indian status when she married a white man.[6] For the same reason, the family was not permitted to reside on the reserve, and contacts were restricted to visits to family and friends and to annual fall fairs.

The Indian side of my family tree was filled with more sinners than saints, and hence was inherently more interesting. My grandmother, Edna Benson, fell into the sinner category. Born in 1900, she was intelligent, quick thinking, and ruthless. When my mother was a little girl in the 1920s, the family dog once returned to the family campsite, jaws red with a sheep's blood. Edna grabbed a burlap bag and hurried to the site of the carnage to stuff the savaged animal into the sack before it could be found by the farmer, who would have called the police. With the help of my mother, she then dragged the carcass to their canoe and paddled to the middle of the lake to tip the bag into the deep.

Fearless, she was the person called upon by neighbours on the reserve to prepare the dead for burial. Possessed by demons that made her violent whether sober or drunk, Edna was ready to do battle with fists and tongue with any man, woman, or representative of the law who crossed her. Cheap sweet wine of the type favoured by skid-row drunks was her drink of preference; rowdy parties complete with quarrelling and brawling were her favourite entertainment. Her own family was not spared; she used to take one of my mother's younger brothers on shoplifting expeditions to stores in Orillia, and she would beat my mother mercilessly for the most minor of transgressions. Once she drove my mother into the river in front of the Indian Camp, where, to her revulsion, a huge black water snake wrapped itself around her body. Edna inherited a house and a sixty-acre sugarbush from her war-hero father, but she squandered what was, to a reserve resident in the 1930s, a fortune. Her relationship with Ed Simcoe was tumultuous; she left him and her children frequently, finally abandoning her family when my mother was only thirteen.

Afraid of Edna's influence, and anxious not to offend her white mother-in-law, who abhorred strong drink and had little use for those who consumed it, my mother refused to allow us children to see our Indian grandmother. I met her only once. Bob and I had been visiting our white grandmother in Orillia when we became embroiled in a nasty stone-throwing escapade with some Orillia boys, whose ranks swelled as the battle raged. Bob and I beat a retreat, fleeing homeward with the pack of Orillia boys in pursuit. Suddenly a lady appeared on the sidewalk and, brandishing a kitchen chair at our tormenters, drove them away with a selection of choice epithets. Bob and I were impressed and grateful. The lady greeted us warmly, announced that she was our granny, and gave us each a nickel. We rushed home to tell our mother, who was dismayed. We left Orillia the next day, and never saw our Indian grandmother again.

My mother went to great lengths to describe to us her early childhood, including the abuse she had suffered at the hands of her mother, to discourage us from ever seeking to meet her and to help us understand the roots of her depression. For years I assumed that this grandmother was the embodiment of all that was evil in the world. My Indian uncles said that this was not true; she had made her children suffer, they said, but that was long ago in a different age. They had forgiven her long before. My mother rebuffed our grandmother's efforts to re-establish ties over the years, telling us that she had never stopped loving her, but could never pardon her behaviour. This was undoubtedly true, but I suspect that my mother was like many Aboriginal women who, having married white men, felt under an unspoken moral pressure to cut or limit their ties to their Native families as a price for acceptance in the white world.

Edna's father, and my great-grandfather, Fred Benson, was a descendant of the Nanegeshkung[7] and Bigwin families and his clan totem was the deer. Fred married Phoebe Snake from the Georgina Island reserve on Lake Simcoe and served in the First World War. Gassed while fighting in northern France in 1917, he was in constant pain from his burnt-out lungs, and continued to cough up blood until he died in the 1930s.

John Bigwin (also known as John Big Wind), honorary chief of the Mnjikaning Indians in the late nineteenth and early twentieth centuries, and *showda* or "uncle" to my grandmother and mother, was the most illustrious member of my mother's extended family. A frequent visitor in the 1920s and 1930s to my mother's home on the Mnjikaning reserve and to the family shack at the Port Carling Indian Camp, he played a central role in family events such as weddings and funerals. The traditional hunting grounds of the Bigwins were actually in the Lake of Bays area of Muskoka; Bigwin Inn, the largest of the grand hotels before it was destroyed by fire a generation ago, was named after his father and constructed on the traditional campsite. He was one of the champions of Indian rights in Ontario in his day, making frequent court appearances to defend the right of Native people to hunt and fish throughout the year; at the turn of the century he even went to London as a Diamond Jubilee guest of Queen Victoria. He was accordingly held in the highest esteem by my mother and by other Native people of her generation, and serves as a role model even today for young Aboriginal people.

My Indian grandfather, Ed Simcoe, was a fisherman and trapper, and worked as a guide for the surveying parties that delineated the Ontario-Manitoba border. An excellent wrestler and tireless runner in his youth, he never recovered from injuries sustained in a chemical explosion at a munitions plant in Nobel, near Parry Sound, in 1916, and died at an early age in 1948. Often in those first years at Port Carling my mother took us four children to see our grandfather, distinguished looking with his weather-beaten face, grey eyes, and silver hair, at his Indian Camp shack, which smelled of sweetgrass, smoke, and fried fish. He was at peace with himself and the world, despite being poor and having endured a lifetime deprived of the civil and political rights enjoyed by white Canadians—never, for example, having been allowed to vote[8] in federal or provincial elections, and even denied the right accorded to other Canadians to purchase beer and spirits.

I would think of my grandfather later in life when I sought contact with Native peoples during my assignments in Latin America, South Africa, and Australia. The condition of the people was terrible. I met Indians in Colombia on the banks of the Casanare River, a tributary of the Orinoco, who were still being hunted for sport on weekends by ranchers who were moving onto their lands. In South Africa I was embarrassed for dispossessed Bushmen who hurriedly undressed to appear naked and thus more "authentic" to busloads of camera-clicking European tourists in search of evidence of a dying culture. In Australia I spoke to Aborigines torn from their families as children, never to see their parents again, and sent to residential schools to be turned into "whites."

3

My grandfather was the son of Nancy Simcoe, who had two other sons who sold fancywork at the Indian Camp. Nancy, who never married, and ruled her family as a bad-tempered despot, took an early dislike to her daughter-in-law and granddaughter. One of my mother's earliest memories, from the early 1930s, is of her grandmother, with her fine-featured face, being carried to her shack by white cottagers who had run over her canoe with their speedboat on Minnahaha Bay at Port Carling. Nancy's hands were mangled and she could no longer see, but she was not taken to hospital. Her broken bones healed, but she remained blind for the rest of her life. In those days, legal recourse was beyond the means of most Aboriginal people, and all she received in compensation was a new canoe and 100 dollars. Despite her handicap, she continued to produce baskets and moccasins of high quality to sell to tourists, working throughout the cool of the night while the other members of the family slept. Her blindness made her, if anything, even more cruel to my mother, who was pressed into service from the age of five to paddle a canoe or lead her grandmother on foot to tourist cottages to sell fancywork.

My mother, Maureen Benson Simcoe, was born in August 1922 at Redwood, close to Port Carling, during a fishing trip on Lake Joseph; her early childhood was spent shuttling back and forth between Mnjikaning and the Indian Camp. Early each spring, her parents would take the train from Mnjikaning to Muskoka Landing, at Gravenhurst on

Lake Muskoka, where her father kept a canoe; they would then paddle thirty kilometres to their cabin at the Indian Camp. In the 1920s her parents spent most of their summers camping on Yoho Island, on Lake Joseph, the site of an Aboriginal settlement in the early 1800s. Her father would trap and fish, often out of season, while her mother would make fancywork to sell to the tourists. Lake trout and bannock (a traditional Indian bread made from a fried or baked mixture of flour, lard, and baking soda) formed the basis of their diet. When it was available, venison, beaver, partridge, and muskrat supplemented their food supply; roast muskrat brains were a particular delicacy.

In late fall they would make the return trip to Mnjikaning. Like many Indian children of the day, my mother received little in the way of formal education. She attended the village school in Port Carling in spring and fall and the Mnjikaning reserve school in winter. Conspicuous in her Native-style long dress and high laced boots, she was the butt of racism far worse than that which Bob and I experienced twenty years later. She became friends with some of her white classmates, though, and that would stand her in good stead when she returned with her family in the mid-1940s.

The reserve school was scarcely better than the one at Port Carling. While obviously not the object of racism from the other children, she was forbidden to speak Chippewa even in the schoolyard and, like her classmates, was often punished for defying the misguided orders of her teachers, whose goal was to foster the assimilation of Native children into mainstream society. My mother was finally forced by her mother to drop out, at the age of eleven, to help out at home; by this time, however, she had acquired a good grasp of reading, writing, and elementary mathematics.

When my Indian grandmother deserted her family, my mother was left to care for her four younger brothers and sisters, until the Indian Agent[9] stepped in to arrange adoptions. One family at Mnjikaning took one brother, and another, from the Moose Deer Point Potawatami[10] reserve on Georgian Bay, accepted a sister. Two brothers remained with their father; my mother lived on her own, doing housework to pay for her keep, until she married my father a year later.

4

The attitude of the people of Port Carling to the Indians who appeared every summer at their traditional campsite was probably neither better nor worse than that displayed by mainstream Canadian society to Native Canadians throughout most of the country's history. There could be instances of compassion. In the late fall of 1927, my Indian grandparents, my mother (then just four), and her brother of nine months, Dalton Lywood, were living at the Indian Camp long after the other Indians had returned to Mnjikaning for the winter. Dalton contracted pneumonia and died. Although my grandparents had no connection with the Anglican church, the priest in Port Carling took matters in hand and arranged a dignified funeral, with six little white boys serving as pallbearers. Dalton was then hurriedly buried before the ground froze at the Port Carling cemetery, in a pauper's grave among those of the white pioneers, in a coffin provided as a gift by carpenters from the village.

No one, however, wanted to be reminded that Port Carling had once been Obogawanung. Some white men fantasized that the Indian Camp was a centre of sin and debauchery, and occasionally ventured down to try to seduce

Indian girls; the Indian men would administer severe drub-
bings and throw the interlopers out of the camp. Contacts
between Indians and villagers were few; indifference, suspicion, distrust, and a tinge of fear predominated, for the divide
was great. Port Carling was a model Anglo-Canadian community; the Indian Camp was an unwanted intrusion of the
Third World into this paradise.

Neither Margaret Laurence nor Robertson Davies
would have been able to find a more archetypical small
Canadian town for their novels than Port Carling, with
maple-lined streets named after the early pioneers, a memori-
al hall, three well-attended Protestant churches whose bells
rang before and after Sunday services, a carefully tended
cemetery, a softball diamond, a Canadian Legion Hall, a
municipal park, a covered skating rink with natural ice, a
library, schools, grocery stores, a boat works that produced
small inboard runabouts, and the Lions Club and the
Imperial Order of the Daughters of the Empire. Margaret
Atwood would have been happy with the potential mystique
of its northern location, where the Precambrian Shield meets
Old Ontario, on the Indian River at the hub of three magnificent lakes. For the convenience of the summer residents, there
was also a restaurant open every July and August, as well as
summer performances by the "Straw Hat Players," featuring
the best of live theatre, with up-and-coming stars such as
Robert Goulet and Donald Sutherland.

The Indians had no potential literary champion. Their
houses were small cabins without electricity that they
described as shacks. In 1946 one water tap and a line of outdoor privies on a hill served the fifty to sixty people who
lived in the community. The York, Schilling, Anderson, Snake,
Williams, Douglas, St. Germain, Laforce, Rennie, and Roads

families are those I remember best (their names reflecting intermarriage dating back 300 years with French *coureurs du bois*, or the cultural influence of the British and American pioneers who crowded them off their lands in the nineteenth century). Relatives from the extended Simcoe family were the most numerous, occupying five shacks in a section informally known as "Simcoe Corners." These shacks were basically for summer use, although a few people, including my grandfather and Sam Williams, occasionally spent a winter there.

In contrast to Port Carling, the Indian Camp was an oasis of peace—most of the time. The ground was carpeted with pine needles and the air was filled with the perfume of giant white pines. The cabins exuded the fragrance of sweetgrass, fresh birchbark, and strips of white ash that were used for making baskets. The Chippewa language is, by its very nature, soft, and conversations were in muted tones. Saturday nights, with their roaring parties, were enlivened by brawls between young Chippewas (always including one of my uncles) and Mohawks, as some vague memory of ancient wars between the two peoples surfaced.

5

The Indians were brown and spoke either Chippewa or Mohawk. The men spent their days fishing on the Muskoka Lakes, trapping, helping their wives produce fancywork, or simply sitting on benches at the public docks. They had belief systems that were alien in some respects to those of their Port Carling neighbours. Most were Christian and churchgoers; some, however, put their faith in guardian spirits that could be called upon for protection in times of need. In pre-Christian times, a guardian spirit was acquired through a vision quest, and was an animal spirit. In Mnjikaning, the spirit was that of a cherished dead relative. My mother held that an uncle who died of malnutrition in the early 1940s was my guardian spirit.

The Indians also believed in water monsters, one of which was understood to reside in Lake Muskoka. My Indian grandfather never failed to seek to appease this creature by leaving small offerings of tobacco at the northern end of Idlewild Island, at a sacred rock that had the form of an Indian head. I recall a cousin coming trembling to our home to tell us that a monster had just emerged from the water right next to his canoe. He never fished in Lake Muskoka again. Even my own father, a self-declared atheist, made propitiatory offerings at the site during fishing trips with my brother and me.

In these early years I spent most of my free time at the Indian Camp; a number of the children were my age and let me read their treasure troves of comic books. My Mohawk friends would impress me with their stories of life in New York, where their fathers were specialists in skyscraper construction. We youngsters would dive for coins that tourists would toss into the water from their motor launches, and we would often go to the Muskoka Lakes Golf and Country Club to caddy. Some of the Indian ladies occasionally pressed me into service to sell quill boxes and moccasins on the main street of Port Carling. I also developed a small business on the side, hunting porcupines for their quills to sell at the Indian camp.

6

A high proportion of the men from Mnjikaning were volunteers in the First and Second World Wars; they were involved in some of the heaviest fighting, and numbers of them were killed and wounded. My Indian great-grandfather, who died on returning to the reserve, and my white great-uncle, who was killed in northern France, were family heroes. I would sit for hours at a time with a distant cousin, Bill Simcoe, on a bench at the public docks, and listen to him describe life in the trenches in France as a sniper and forward artillery observer, radioing-in coordinates in Chippewa to another member of the reserve to confuse the enemy. The scenes he painted of mindless carnage and destruction on another continent in another age seemed so remote from his quiet life as a trapper that they sounded like science fiction. His ever-present crutches, and the flapping pant leg covering the limb he lost at the hip in 1916, indicated otherwise. I also heard accounts of fighting in France, Belgium, and Holland from Ivan Douglas, wounded in northwestern Germany in 1945. Ivan once showed me his shrapnel scars, saying that young people had a responsibility to eliminate the causes of war. He strongly criticized those who sought to glorify conflict, saying such people obviously could never have fought in a war.

Bill Simcoe refused to wear an artificial leg, and it never would have crossed his mind to don a life vest while fishing. He was a superb paddler; in the spring, when the water was high from the snowmelt, he would plunge his canoe through an open sluice gate at the Port Carling dam and run the rapids of the Indian River. Ivan Douglas and his wife, Peggy, an Algonquin from the Golden Lake reserve near Renfrew, Ontario, were close friends of my parents, who would visit them often at their home at Mnjikaning. Ivan was elected Chief of the reserve, but he died at an early age at the Sunnybrook Hospital for Veterans in Toronto after much suffering from his war wounds. Peggy passed away shortly thereafter.

Many years later, when I accompanied Prime Minister Chrétien to Europe on the fiftieth anniversary of the Normandy landings, I told him about the sacrifice that so many Native Canadians had made in defence of Canada in the world wars. The prime minister's speech, broadcast live across Canada from the Bény-sur-Mer Commonwealth War Cemetery, where the Canadian war dead from Juno Beach and the battle for Caen are buried, accordingly made prominent reference to the wartime contribution of Canada's Native community in general and to that of Mnjikaning in particular. He singled out Ivan Douglas and Sanford Stinson, another reserve resident and a childhood friend of my mother, killed while fighting as a member of the Sherbrooke Fusiliers in Normandy in July 1944.

Great-grandfather Shields predicted that the author would "follow in his footsteps" as a backwoods preacher.

Four
White Roots

Out of the crooked timber of humanity, no straight thing was ever made.
　　　— Kant, as quoted by Isaiah Berlin

1

My white grandparents stepped in at this time to provide decisive moral support, visiting us frequently and eventually moving to Port Carling to live beside us in a modest cabin constructed next to our home. While they could not help us financially and detested each other, they were devoted to their grandchildren and spent an enormous amount of time passing on stories of their families in days long past, doing their part to impart values for us to take into the world.

　　My grandfather, William Bain Bartleman, emigrated at the turn of the century from the Scottish Highland town of Ballater, the site of Balmoral Castle, the estate of the royal family near Aberdeen. His father, James, kept a grocery store at the Ballater railway station and was one of the local suppliers to the royal family. My grandfather used to regale me with stories of delivering groceries to the kitchen door of the Castle, of his trips to illegal whisky stills in the Highlands, and of watching royalty from across Europe, including the Russian tsar and the German kaiser, disembark at the quiet railway station to be greeted by Queen Victoria in the dying days of the nineteenth century.

William and his two brothers came to Canada as part of the massive movement of young Britons at the turn of the century. Their parents paid their fares to Galt (now Cambridge), Ontario, and then they were on their own. One, who had become a journalist, was killed in 1917 while serving with the Canadian Highland Light Infantry in the battles for Hill 70, preparatory to the battle for Vimy Ridge, and is buried in the Commonwealth War Cemetery at Lens. The other was wounded in the same battle, but he survived to become a major in the Canadian army in the Second World War. With five children, my grandfather obtained a deferment, for which my grandmother was still reproaching him fifty years later.

Like my own father, my grandfather William was an avid reader and a dreamer. He worked as a moulder in various foundries around Ontario; his pay was poor, and he was unemployed for long periods during the Great Depression. His passion was socialism; he felt strongly about the need to correct social and economic injustices and was without an ounce of racial prejudice. He fought to introduce trade unionism into the factories where he worked, was often elected shop steward, and for many years was a member of the Workmen's Compensation Board in Orillia. My relations with him were extremely close, and he exerted an enormous influence on me in my formative years with his strong egalitarian ideals.

William married Margaret Shields and raised five children, my father being the second eldest. Margaret ruled her family (including my mother) as a selfless, loving, but fiery and opinionated matriarch, and was strongly spiritual. Proud of her roots, she never tired of describing how her great-grandmother, Anne Kay of Brownlow House, County

Armagh, Ireland, eloped to Canada in the 1820s with Bill White, steward to Lord Brownlow, to become pioneers in Upper Canada. On special occasions she could be persuaded to describe how members of this branch of the family had become strong supporters of the reform movement and William Lyon Mackenzie in the Rebellion of 1837.[11] She would then repeat a story that had been in the family for generations; it told how the Whites had sheltered Mackenzie himself, hiding him under a pile of shavings in a workshop before he fled on horseback to the United States with the law on his trail, after the failed attack on the British forces at Montgomery's Tavern on Yonge Street. In a twist of fate, Indian ancestors of my mother from the Lake Simcoe area were on the other side in the conflict, mobilized by the lieutenant governor, Sir George Arthur, to help put down the rebellion and assist in protecting the colony from raids by Mackenzie's defeated forces in 1838.

Margaret's father, my great-grandfather, John Shields, was the eldest son of a prosperous farmer, but renounced his inheritance to become an itinerant preacher in the backwoods of the province. Although in his nineties, he used to come to Port Carling to hold open-air religious services, highlighted by lengthy prayers in English and hymn singing in Chippewa, at the Indian Camp. Dressed in their best clothes, the people would wait expectantly among the pine trees for the service to begin. My great-grandfather, handsome and with a shock of white hair, looking every inch the patriarch, would begin to speak. The Indians, who enjoyed a good sermon, would be appreciative—at least for a while. My great-grandfather had an extraordinary memory and knew the Old and New Testaments by heart. Quoting the Bible at length, he would lose track of time as he reminded the Native congregation that according to his religion, the Indians of America were the lost tribes of Israel. I don't think this unduly impressed the worshippers, the majority of whom were members of the United Church, and they would become restless. From time to time he would stop preaching to allow a hymn to be sung. That was what everyone was waiting for. The music was unlike anything my young ears had ever heard; although the hymns were standard ones, their rendition in Chippewa was extraordinarily beautiful.

I had nothing but respect for my famous great-grandfather, an opinion not shared by my father, who loathed him for his religion, for his teetotal habits, and for disciplining him with a razor strop when he was young. To provoke and, in the process, to obtain revenge, my father would get roaring drunk on homemade raisin wine and sleep in a hutch with my pet rabbits every time my great-grandfather came to stay at our home.

2

God, my great-grandfather told me, had chosen me to succeed him as a preacher. As a result of the death of my playmate on the Dump Road, I had already started asking myself the type of question only children dare raise. What happens when someone dies? Is there really a soul? Is there really a God? How was the world created? Can something be created out of nothing? Who could disprove the Indian belief that the wind, water, trees, rocks, and all parts of the physical world were inhabited by spirits, good and bad?

My great-grandfather's prediction accentuated this sense of wonder and precipitated much soul-searching and some terrifying dreams, as I sought to come to terms with these universal questions. In contrast to the other youngsters of the village, who came from families with solidly Christian religious backgrounds, and who never, to my knowledge, ever questioned the articles of their inherited faith, my family was deeply divided. My father was a vociferous atheist; my white grandfather was a quiet sceptic; my white grandmother was deeply religious; my great-grandfather was a charismatic Christian; and my mother did not take sides.

To confuse matters even more, my Indian relatives, while nominally Christian, believed in devils and water monsters. One, from the same generation as my white great-grandfather, was feared as a devil on the reserve (my mother told me that he was, in fact, a quiet old man with a spiritual bent). I came to the conclusion that the beliefs of the Indians and the Christianity of the villagers were emanations of the same religious impulse. If I rejected the former on the grounds that the Indian beliefs were simple superstition, logic told me that I had to reject Christianity as well, since it arose from the same source.

A turning point occurred early. I remember playing with Bob in our front yard, swinging and spinning on a rope tied to a branch on an apple tree. It was a glorious day in late May and the blossoms were in full flower. The thought came to me in ecstasy that all of this joy was destined to end; the cycle of life would play itself out, but I would never find the answers to the questions I was asking myself. I stopped being a child at that moment.

I derived no comfort from this insight, however, and, in the hope that a flash of illumination would occur, attended Sunday School and church services at the Port Carling United

Church regularly until I was twelve, and tried a variety of churches at university. I resumed my quest in the course of my subsequent diplomatic career, attending religious ceremonies and meeting holy men in Latin America, Asia, Africa, and Europe. In Bangladesh in the early 1970s I visited mosques, talked to mullahs, and attended Muslim services at which tens of thousands of the faithful prayed to Allah. In Israel in the 1980s I called on leading rabbis. I also met priests and monks and visited the Church of the Nativity in Bethlehem and the Church of the Holy Sepulchre in Jerusalem, the traditional sites of Christ's birth and burial respectively. In the 1990s, during visits to the Vatican, I tried to discern in the eyes of the Pope and his senior archbishops the basis of their faith. In New York's Harlem, I took my family to a black charismatic religious service.

My hope that exposure to the fervour of others would provide answers has not been realized, but searches of this kind never end. I have remained comfortable at the intuitive level with the Aboriginal belief that the world has always existed and always will. I sense the numinous in the big drum of the powwow celebrations, in quiet places, and in the art of Native peoples, whether ancient rock engravings or X-ray paintings of artists of today. The art of the Southern African Bushman and the Aborigines of Australia, which Marie-Jeanne and I came to know so well during our postings to those countries, conveyed exactly the same message, at least to me. My great-grandfather would have been disappointed to learn of his great-grandson's spiritual path; certainly my white grandmother was, and told me so before she died.

3

My relations with my father were ambivalent during those years. On the one hand, he confided in me at an early age that, while never a member of the Communist Party, he had named me James Karl after Karl Marx. This revelation fascinated and alarmed me in equal measure. My father had revealed himself to me as someone who believed in social justice even if he had been temporarily attracted by a dangerous and unorthodox means of seeking to achieve it. Although dating from his youth and long since abandoned, these sympathies, had they become known in the McCarthyite period, would have meant instant ostracism for our family in a staunchly conservative village where communism was equated with the anti-Christ. His admission to me was to be our secret, binding us together in a pact of father-son complicity until I left the village for good.

He also allowed me to accompany him on his frequent visits to the Public Library, and my voracious appetite for books and reading was probably influenced by his example. In addition to stories of his life as a hobo, he repeated at great length the contents of books on history and travel that he had read. Aboriginal history was his favourite subject, and he never tired of recounting the lives of early explorers and fur traders and their interaction with Canada's Native peoples. He was ahead of his time in not believing in corporal punishment, never in his life raising his hand against any of his children. My mother, who did not share these scruples, wasn't averse to giving her children a good hiding from time to time when we deserved it.

On the other hand, he followed the old Scottish habit of never displaying emotion to his children. Likewise, he assumed that the four Bartleman children would probably follow the lead of their parents and drop out of school at an early age. It would not have occurred to him to praise any of us for doing well at school. My father more than compensated for this neglect by inculcating in us children a love for nature from our earliest years, taking us on fishing and blueberry-picking expeditions and attempting to persuade us not to follow the example of our friends in their mindless killing of every snake and frog they encountered.

Our relationship in the matter of race was more problematic. Occasionally, furious at me for some peccadillo, he would tell me that unless I was careful I would grow up to be a shiftless Indian. This would render me speechless with a rage mixed with helplessness, guilt, and fear. Rage came from a profound feeling that my father's comment was deeply unjust to my mother, to my brother and sisters, and to all Indians. Helplessness and fear came from a suspicion that perhaps my father was right; could it be that my Indian blood had condemned me to come to no good, no matter what I did in life? My white grandmother, despite her deep affection for me, raised further doubts by telling me at an early age that there was something in my face that made her think I was destined to be an alcoholic.

I wrestled with these thoughts throughout adolescence and into adulthood, eventually coming to the conclusion that my father and my beloved grandmother had been spouting nonsense. Nevertheless, on the deeper level where nightmares reside, a seed of doubt was planted; perhaps my life was somehow genetically predestined to failure. I also puzzled over how it was possible for individuals and people to love and to hate, to admire and to disdain, and to value and to deprecate each other all at the same time. Thirty-five years in the foreign service in Europe, Asia, the Middle East, Latin America, and Africa has led me to suspect that suffering is caused as often by decisions taken casually and indifferently as it is by hatred, jealousy, rivalry, and fear.

In December 1995, for example, at the Commonwealth heads of government meeting in Christchurch, New Zealand, I listened with great embarrassment as a Canadian journalist, anxious to get a good quote for his newspaper, asked the son of Ken Saro-Wiwa, the great Nigerian poet and defender of human rights under sentence of death in a Nigerian prison, to speculate on the exact techniques his executioners would use to kill his father. Would they, he asked the son, who was emerging from a meeting with the Canadian prime minister, hang his father or shoot him? How would he react when he received the news? The son just stared at the witless journalist, aware that his father was being led to the gallows as they talked.

During the Intifada of the late 1980s, a group of Canadian parliamentarians on a private visit to Israel insisted that I give them a tour of Palestinian refugee camps under curfew and United Nations hospitals filled with the wounded; they wanted to witness Palestinians clashing with Israeli soldiers and to see what live ammunition and rubber bullets could do to human flesh. I eventually realized that my guests were actually engaged in a type of disaster tourism, obtaining their thrills from seeing violence and suffering at first hand, with Canada's ambassador as their tour guide.

At the NATO summit in Rome in November 1991, I listened from my privileged place in the conference room as

President Mitterand of France, President George Bush Senior of the United States, Chancellor Kohl of Germany, and a variety of prime ministers, including John Major of the United Kingdom and Felipe Gonzales of Spain, passionately discussed the security architecture of the Europe that was emerging from the Cold War. As they talked, the Yugoslav Serb army was systematically destroying Dubrovnik on the Adriatic coast, less than an hour away by air. The NATO leaders eventually turned their attention to the mayhem being committed on their doorstep, but confined their action to issuing a pious communiqué requesting that the Serbs halt their depredations. The Serbs could recognize indifference. They ravaged the world heritage site and then turned their attention to Bosnia.

I found it hard to judge these displays of callous apathy, for I, during my first posting abroad, had been as guilty in my personal behaviour as the journalist, the politicians, and the NATO leaders in theirs. Shortly after arriving in Bogota, Colombia, in February 1968 as a third secretary[11] in the Canadian embassy, I was invited to dinner at a restaurant by Colombian colleagues at the mission. After the meal, my new friends undertook to walk with me to my apartment. We emerged joking and laughing into the gloom of a typical Bogota evening. It was cold and a light rain was falling. Circles of light illuminated patches of sidewalk directly under the widely spaced streetlights; in between, it was dark. Two streetlights from the restaurant, we came across a child no more than three years old lying on the cement, tears flowing from his eyes, his hands grasping his stomach, moaning from pain and loneliness. Despite the cold and rain, he was dressed only in a light shirt and shorts; he had no socks or shoes.

If only I could live my life again and do the right thing this time. To my shame, I heeded the advice of my companions to do nothing. They said that no hospital or refuge would accept the child, who obviously had been abandoned by his mother to join the army of street children in the city. I stepped around him and continued on my way.

The author returns from raking leaves and washing windows for summer residents in the early 1950s.

Five
The Fisherman

This is a plain account of a fishing party. It is not a story. There is no plot. Nothing happens in it and nobody gets hurt. The only point of this narrative is its particular truth.
  — Stephen Leacock, *The Old, Old Story of How Five Men Went Fishing*

1

Expected to contribute to my keep, I became successively a *Globe and Mail*, *Toronto Star*, and *Toronto Telegram* carrier boy between the ages of eight and thirteen. The village was extensive, the houses were set far apart, and I never had more than thirty customers. I was an indifferent entrepreneur, spending most of my earnings as a newspaper carrier boy on comic books and ice cream cones, often leaving my mother to pay the circulation managers. On the other hand, I used my paper route to supplement the family income by taking orders for fish, illegally gill-netted by my father, and delivering them, wrapped in old newspapers and hidden in my carrier bag.

Our small family fishing venture started when my father acquired an old net from the trucker for whom he worked. Under the attentive eyes of his two sons, my father mended the worst of the holes and then set about making proper sinkers. It was a mild spring day in 1948 when this labour of love began. Bob and I were in charge of starting and maintaining a bonfire in our backyard, made muddy by water from melting snow that trickled down the steep hill behind our house. There were buds but not yet leaves on the trees, the Muskoka air was soft and warm, crows and seagulls making their first appearance in force after wintering in the south were calling to each other, and the Indian River glistened in the distance.

My father tossed a collection of old lead pipes into a rusty cast-iron pot, which we placed over the roaring fire. When the lead melted, Bob and I helped him remove the cauldron from the fire and pour its contents into a series of sand moulds fashioned to form large circular sinkers. My father attached the sinkers along one side of the sixty-foot-long net and fixed wooden floats along the other. We were now ready for some illicit fishing.

Bob and I were willing accomplices. Although less than ten years old, we sometimes accompanied him on his nighttime forays. There was always an air of excitement and danger. The penalty for being caught fishing with a gill net was harsh: 1,000 dollars and the confiscation of boat and vehicle. My father did not have the money to own a car or truck, but with a weekly wage of forty dollars, he would not have been able to pay the fine had we been caught, and would probably have gone to jail.

We would wait for moonless nights with cloud cover to mask the starlight and then walk through the dark to our canoe at the water's edge, with only the occasional spark from my father's pipe betraying our presence. My father would take the net out of a large packsack and place it in the canoe. We would push quietly out into the current, never removing our paddles from the water, to avoid making splashing sounds, and propel our canoe along until we reached a good spot to set the net. My father would return alone in the early hours to haul in the fish while the family slept.

Our clandestine fishing business came to an abrupt end when the game warden, tipped off that illegal fishing was going on, raided the house of a neighbour early one fall evening. My mother saw the flashing lights of his vehicle and warned my father, who grabbed the packsack containing the net and ran to hide it in the thick bush behind our house. It turned out that our neighbour was also fishing illegally. The game warden was so happy to have bagged someone, complete with all the necessary evidence, that he did not come to our house.

But my mother had had enough. The net had to go. Fortunately, one of her Mnjikaning relatives, who was often an uninvited guest at our house, especially at dinner time, asked to borrow our unwanted treasure. The relative had a fierce temper and became dangerous when drinking. Some years before, during a fight in the family home on the reserve, he had knocked his brother against the stove, spilling a tub of boiling water over his body. The young man staggered to the home of my mother, who was then a young girl, to seek help. The victim entered the house and wordlessly raised his shirt to reveal his badly burnt torso before collapsing. Some months before, his cousin had been hanged at the regional jail at Whitby for murdering a night watchman at a factory in Orillia. The father, afraid that his offending son would suffer the same fate, appealed to the victim to tell the RCMP (which policed all Indian reserves in those days) that he had been accidentally scalded.

The brother died and our unwanted guest escaped the hangman, but my mother did not want him around her children. I did not like him, because he would tell us stories of close encounters with the Windigo, the cannibalistic devil of

Chippewa folklore, which scared me witless.

As expected, after he borrowed the net we never saw him or the net again.

2

Net or no net, I harboured a passion for fishing, but had neither natural talent nor luck. For example, at the beginning of the summer of 1952 I resolved to hire a float plane from Redwing Flying Services, located on Lake Rosseau near the Muskoka Lakes Golf and Country Club, to fly to a small lake near Georgian Bay reputed to hold giant pike. Jerry, my best friend in my adolescent years, immediately agreed to join the expedition and to share the costs.

In those years Jerry and I were inseparable, hunting, fishing, picking berries, pursuing girls, and collecting scrap metal to sell to a dealer in Orillia. We were not above becoming involved in a variety of pranks—once creeping at night through the bush to a gathering of young summer visitors who were telling each other hair-raising stories around their wilderness campfire. We added realism to their evening's entertainment by emitting bloodcurdling howls out of the darkness, stampeding the entire contingent down a pitch-black trail to seek refuge with their parents, who were comfortably ensconced in their luxury lodgings. On Halloween, we joined other adolescents from the village in overturning outdoor toilets, scrawling graffiti in soap on car windows, and decorating trees and telephone lines with toilet paper liberated from the school storeroom.

Jerry was thus the perfect companion for the fishing adventure. Neither of us had any money, but that did not deter the intrepid twelve-year-olds that we were. To raise the fifty dollars required to pay the pilot to fly us to our destination and pick us up a week later, as soon as school was out at the end of June we appeared every morning at the caddy shack of the golf club seeking employment. The financial returns were unimpressive. The rich tourists for whom we carried golf bags almost as large as ourselves paid us only sixty cents for nine holes, or one dollar for eighteen. We were occasionally given ten-cent tips. By the middle of July we had managed to save only five dollars between us. Comic books and ice cream cones had eaten seriously into our meagre take. We resolved to go underground and earn our fortune as illicit golf ball hunters and sellers.

The club had a strict rule that golf balls, used or new, could only be sold at the caddy shack. All lost balls were regarded as the property of the golf club itself. Any caddy who turned in balls found in the course of his duties could expect to be paid a pittance; the balls were resold with a 300-percent mark-up. Jerry considered this to be unfair, and I, having listened to my father decry the capitalist exploitation of the working class, also firmly believed it to be part of a system that had to be fought. Besides, we could make a lot of money if we played our cards right.

We noted that the club manager rarely left the confines of the clubhouse, spending his time drinking at the bar, socializing with members, and playing jazz and blues hour after hour at the piano. We reckoned he would not notice if we started our own little business on the 520-yard fifth hole, the longest on the course and the farthest point from the caddy shack.

Therefore every day until late August, Jerry and I hitchhiked or walked the two miles from Port Carling to the prestigious golf club, but instead of reporting for duty as victimized caddies, we disappeared into the bush. We would thoroughly scour the sides of the fairways, and collect an average of twenty balls every day. Jerry, with his keen eyesight, always found more than I, although I excelled in recovering balls in the mud. With my shoes and socks removed and my pant legs rolled up, I delighted in searching for golf balls in the mucky water of the creeks that cut across the third fairway and ran alongside the fifth. I loved the feel of warm mud oozing between my toes, the smell of rotting vegetation, and the heat of the sun on my back. Whenever my toes locked onto a hard round object, I experienced the high a professional gambler gets when he hits the jackpot. Around 11:00 each morning we would lie in wait for our clientele on the fifth tee, located at the top of a steep trail. Jerry entrusted me to take the lead in the negotiations.

I would emerge from the bushes and, after ascertaining that my intended prey was not the manager of the club, sidle up to some stockbroker from Toronto or Hamilton panting his way to the top of the hill. "Wanna buy some golf balls, mister?" I would haggle over the prices. I knew golf balls and drove a hard bargain, sometimes obtaining more for a used ball than its price when new. I was to recognize myself myriad times in years to come when street urchins in Bogota, Dacca, New Delhi, Mexico City, Cairo, and dozens of other cities would approach me on the street with wares to offload.

Jerry and I cleared five dollars a day. Occasionally the manager would emerge from the clubhouse and try to catch us, but he did not have a chance. We would slip into the bush, which we knew like the backs of our hands, leaving him fuming on the fairway and threatening us with the law. But he never called the police. He was married to a girl from Port Carling and, I believe, secretly admired our inventiveness.

By the middle of August we had more than enough money to pay for the flights to and from our dream lake. It was just as well, since our market for golf balls had dried up—most tourists in those days abandoned Muskoka to attend the Canadian National Exhibition in Toronto, which always opened at that time. We bought provisions, extra fishing gear, and everything else we expected we would need for our one-week expedition in the wilds. In the last week of August, Red Wing Flying Service flew us, a tent, and a supply of food to our lake. The pilot promised to return to collect us and our anticipated great haul of fish in a week.

We had no luck. Despite fishing from early morning until late at night every day, we did not even get a bite. Jerry, however, had brought along his .22-calibre rifle and an ample supply of ammunition. I forgot the admonition of my father not to kill helpless creatures and joined Jerry in shooting squirrels and birds, in the aimless manner of feckless youth. At one stage, bored with shooting squirrels, Jerry opened fire on an old boat we had found and were using to get from one side of the lake to the other. I was in the boat. Jerry thought it uproariously funny as he pumped shot after shot at the floor near my feet from a distance of thirty feet. I was less amused.

I got my revenge on the third day. We had pulled the boat up onto a bare flat rock bereft of vegetation, which protruded some twelve inches out of the water in the middle of the lake, and were trying our luck once again. Suddenly a monster grabbed my line. Jerry watched intently as I battled the fish. We were both wild with anticipation as I dragged the leviathan up onto the rock. The fish took one look at us, obviously did not like what it saw, casually spat out the hook, and disappeared into the black water.

Instead of becoming discouraged, stout sons of Muskoka that we were, we "knew" that there had to be dozens of giant pike waiting to be caught if only we persevered at this spot. Therefore, at my instigation, we headed for shore, took down our tent, packed it and all our supplies into the boat, and returned to our new campsite, full of enthusiasm.

No matter that we could not erect our tent on a flat rock that could not accommodate anchors for the pegs; we simply spread the canvas and prepared to crawl under it to sleep when necessary. No matter that the sky was turning black, that thunder could be heard off in the distance, and that the wind was beginning to pick up, pushing waves over the edge of our sanctuary. We were tough Muskoka boys, unfazed by the prospect of a mere storm, which to us was only a nuisance compared with the prospect of hauling in giant pike.

Alas, we caught nary a fish. To make matters worse, as afternoon turned to evening, light rain dampened down our roaring campfire, although it did not extinguish it. Then a heavy rain fell, quenching the fire and driving us to shelter. The distant thunderstorm arrived in full fury, with lightning flashing and thunder crashing down on our heads. We cowered under the canvas, thoroughly soaked and chilled to the bone. Worse was to come.

During a break in the storm, I sought to make conversation by relating to my companion recent statistics for lightning deaths in Canada, and noted helpfully that, given our location on an exposed rocky outcrop in the middle of a lake, we were prime targets. I also said that what we were witnessing could well be the tail end of a hurricane that had been threatening Florida several days before we flew to the lake. If so, we could expect more heavy rain and torrential winds. If we survived the night, the weather was sure to be wet and rainy until the pilot returned to rescue us in three days. Jerry told me to shut up.

Unfortunately, I was right. The rain came down in buckets and the wind became even more furious. Waves surged over the rock, swamping our possessions and rolling over the canvas under which we were huddling. I had never been as cold, wet, and miserable, nor would I ever be again. The only experience to rival it occurred forty years later when I was swept out of a boat while salmon fishing on the Eagle River in Labrador, and carried down falls and rapids for more than a kilometre. I didn't catch any fish then either.

Toward dawn the rain slackened to a drizzle, the wind died, and the waves retreated, restricting their pernicious behaviour to slopping over the edge of the island. We crawled out, wet, bitterly cold, tired, and unhappy. After failing to light a fire with the wood that had not been swept away, we bailed out the boat, piled our drenched possessions on board, and headed back to our original campsite to erect our soggy tent and wait in misery until the pilot came back.

On our return to Port Carling we thought it prudent not to mention that Jerry had been taking pot shots at his best friend with his rifle (or indeed that he had even taken a rifle with him) and that I had persuaded my buddy to decamp to an inhospitable rock just before the worst storm of the summer.

Mother and father (Maureen and Percy Bartleman) in Port Carling in the late 1940s.
In the early 1950s: Bob; sisters Mary and Janet; and the author.

Chief John Bigwin, a distant great-uncle of the author and role model for people from Mnjikaning.
Grandfather William Bartleman; Sam Williams; grandmother Margaret Shields.

Indian Village, Port Carling, Muskoka, Canada.

The Indian Camp at Port Carling in the 1920s as the author's mother would have known it. Photo courtesy Muskoka Lakes Museum.

Natives sell fancywork at the Indian Camp at Port Carling as the author knew it. Photo courtesy Muskoka Lakes Museum.

SAGAMO AND CHEROKEE PASSING AT LOCKS.

In the 1940s Whitings Drug Store was a cornucopia of cheap souvenirs, comic books, and ice cream. Photo courtesy Morley Stephens.

Indian Head Rock on Lake Muskoka. The author's Indian grandfather always sought to appease the gods of the lake with offerings of tobacco at this site. Photo courtesy Muskoka Steamship & Historical Society.

Steamboats dock at Port Carling in the early 1930s. The author's future home is the abandoned house on the hill in the background. Photo courtesy Muskoka Steamship & Historical Society.

Sagamo docks at Port Carling in the early 1930s. Photo courtesy Muskoka Steamship & Historical Society.

Louis Armstrong performing in Muskoka in 1963. Photo by the author.
Summer estate "Black Forest," where the author worked for seven summers in
the 1950s and early 1960s. Photo courtesy Nancy Muse.

The author with his "muscle car" in 1960; it did not impress the Big City girls.

The author as a young diplomat (right) sits in on discussions between Prime Minister Sheik Mujibur Rahman (left) and Ivan Head, foreign policy advisor to Prime Minister Trudeau in 1973.

The author as a young ambassador, accompanied by his wife Marie-Jeanne, greeting President Castro at the entrance to the Canadian residence in Cuba in 1981.

The author as foreign policy advisor to Prime Minister Chrétien meets Prime Minister Yitzhak Rabin in New York two weeks before his assassination. Photo courtesy Jean-Marc Carisse.

The author receiving the Aboriginal
National Achievement Award for public
service, from then Premier Roy Romanow
in Regina, Saskatchewan, in 1999.

Father departing for work as lockmaster, while mother prepares for a
day cleaning cottages in the late 1950s.

Seven
Upwardly Mobile

The long call of the loon echoes over the lake. The air is cool and fresh. There is in it all the new life of the land of the silent pine and the moving waters. Lake Wissanotti in the morning sunlight! Don't talk to me of the Italian lakes or the Tyrol or the Swiss Alps. I don't want them.
> — Stephen Leacock, *The Marine Excursion of the Knights of Pythias*

1

By the time I was a teenager, the Bartlemans had been accepted in the village as a hard-working, honest, and racially mixed family that, despite their poverty, had never accepted welfare. My father was starting to fit into the community life as a unique character. Bob, with his dark complexion, was still the occasional object of racist remarks, but defended himself well with his fists when he needed to, and had a fan club of girls who were attracted by his good looks. Having started to do well in school, I acquired some self-confidence. We would soon start to claw our way up the economic ladder and emerge from poverty. Another modest entry in the annals of the Canadian Dream was about to be written.

My mother started to work as a cleaning lady and part-time cook in the homes of a number of tourists. The pay was low but she obtained a steady supply of good quality hand-me-down clothing and used books for her children and established friendly relations with a wide variety of influential people, who were more than willing to do her a favour. She decided that the family would never prosper unless my father obtained a government job, and resolved to use her connections to that end. She was well aware, in those bad old days of political patronage, that local members of provincial parliament (if members of the governing party) were allowed to appoint their own candidates to low-level government jobs in their ridings without competition. She lobbied her employers to write to the local MPP to support my father's candidacy for the position of village lockmaster when it became vacant. The parliamentarian was inundated with letters from prominent Canadians, my father got the job (becoming in the process an overnight, if insincere, convert to the cause of the governing party), and the Bartlemans were lifted out of dire poverty.

In my diplomatic career, the roles would be reversed. After I reached the rank of ambassador, Marie-Jeanne and I would pass on used clothing and books to the hard-working maids and cooks who staffed the various official residences put at our disposal. Occasionally we were able to help in obtaining employment and visas for the children of household staff. Sometimes we established lifetime friendships. In every case, I saw my mother reflected in their faces: black, brown, yellow, or white; male or female. It thus caused me great distress when I saw bad apples in the diplomatic corps exploit their staff, to make them work long hours without compensation, to appropriate for themselves allowances provided by their governments for food for the staff, and to threaten them with dismissal if they complained. Such practices are now a thing of the past in the Canadian Foreign Service but not in others.

In Bangladesh, where I was sent as a young bachelor in the early 1970s to open Canada's first diplomatic mission, the staff were all male; they padded around the modest residence in their bare feet and saved every penny they could to send to their famine-stricken home villages to feed their families. In Cuba, in the early 1980s, there was a mix of male and female, white, black, and in-between; they bonded with our two older children, then just five and six years old respectively, and our departure at the end of our two-year tour was heartbreaking for everyone. In Israel, we met a Filipino couple who were to remain with us for nine years, following us to work at the official residence of the ambassador to NATO when I was transferred to Brussels in 1990. We mourned as members of the family when the husband passed away some years later. In South Africa we grew close to the cook, but not the butler. In Australia we enjoyed the rough and friendly egalitarianism of the household staff. Back in Brussels on our final posting at the beginning of the new millennium, we established firm ties with a staff of Corsicans, Portuguese, Filipinos, and Belgians. I suspect that when we retire we will cherish these people more in our memories than we will our fellow diplomats and our host country contacts.

2

My father decided to celebrate the change in family fortunes by installing an indoor toilet, adding a room on the back, and painting the house. We did the work ourselves. Locating a heavily rusted used septic tank at the village dump, we cleaned it as well as we could and hauled it home on the back of a truck. We then peppered it with shotgun and .22 rifle fire to allow it to leak as much of its contents as possible into the surrounding soil (we didn't have room for a proper tile system) and installed it surreptitiously so as to avoid attracting the attention of the health inspector, who might have questioned the open trench that led straight from the tank to a ditch leading to the river.

Bob and I particularly enjoyed preparing the ground for the addition. Drawing on a stock of dynamite and nitroglycerine caps that our father stored in the house, we blasted rocks and dirt to our hearts' content. Becoming overconfident, we decided to remove a large rock that abutted the cabin of our Bartleman grandparents. However, we miscalculated the charge and blew in the side of the building, which meant we were faced with a major rebuilding job.

My father and I, under the watchful eye of my mother, who knew more about carpentry than we did, erected the new room—neglecting to insulate the floor, which heaved every spring thereafter when the frost left the ground. The job of painting the house was accomplished courtesy of the provincial government. Every night after work until the job was finished, my father would "borrow" a pail of the green stain used on the public docks and buildings, and we would happily apply it to the thirsty exterior of our home. He never worried, although he should have, that suspicions might have been aroused by the trail of green that led from the government storeroom, down the street, and up our walkway to our house, which was, coincidentally enough, freshly stained in government colours.

Despite my father's position as the only public servant (other than the postmaster) in the village, he, and as a consequence our family as a whole, did not move up the social ladder. To be sure, he mastered the art of doing what was expected of a public servant by spending most of the day drinking coffee and delegating the bulk of his work to his assistants. In other respects he was simply too unconventional. He would engage the retired village doctor and other village notables in spirited discussions at the local coffee shop on whether or not there was a God, attack tenets of received wisdom, and do his best to cast doubts into the minds of true believers. He also became more sophisticated in his wine-making techniques, experimenting with different varieties of dried and fresh fruits and berries. Never discouraged by the fact that all his concoctions tasted the same, he added vegetable colouring to make red, green, blue, and brown varieties—highly appreciated by the coterie of village rebels and ne'er-do-wells who joined him in the evenings to sample his *millésimes* and listen to his tall tales.

3

Lest it be thought that my father didn't give a fig for conventional opinion, he finally made an effort—even if his heart wasn't in it—to live up to the expectations associated with his new position in life. He became a regular patron of Straw Hat Players theatre productions and a member of the Library Board. He also acquired a number of horses and ponies, which would live to record ages, and, quietly and without official sanction, constructed a monstrosity of a barn out of scrap lumber on the hill behind our house to accommodate them.

Unfortunately, when it was wet the manure had a habit of sliding down the hill into the backyard of our neighbours, who had opened a restaurant. Their customers did not share our enthusiasm for the fresh smell of the barnyard; they would have been even less happy had they known that the manure pile was also the last resting place for deceased equine friends.

My father had talents other than managerial that were fully exploited by the Ontario Department of Public Works, his official employer. He had a flair for using high explosives, and thus became responsible for all dynamiting jobs around the locks. He prided himself on being able to judge exactly how many sticks of dynamite were required for each job, although the village fathers did complain once when he showered the main business area with rock and debris, almost killing half a dozen tourists in the process.

He also mastered the use of a deep-sea diving suit, and became responsible for underwater repairs at Ontario government establishments throughout Central and Eastern Ontario. His diving days almost came to an early end one day in July 1959, when his loyal assistants at the locks bolted his helmet into place and then sat down to wait for him to descend the fifteen steps into the water before starting to pump air to him. According to their logic, he obviously did not need to breathe until he was under water. Suffocating, nearly unconscious, and hampered by fifty pounds of lead weights in his shoes, my father was crawling in desperation toward the air crank when a passerby saw what was happening and came to his rescue.

4

My father loved his job, particularly meeting and talking to cottagers, opening and closing the swing bridge over the Indian River, and operating the lock-gates to allow steamships to pass from one lake to another. When I was a child in the 1940s, five steamships—the *Sagamo*, the *Segwun*, the *Cherokee*, the *Ahmic*, and the *Islander*—plied the lakes carrying mail, freight, and tourists from Gravenhurst to Port Carling, Bala, and the grand hotels that then dotted the lakes.

In those summers, the morning and evening arrivals of the steamboats at the public docks were highlights of the day. Each steamboat would emit sharp whistle blasts as it approached the locks to alert the lockmaster and his assistant to make ready. Dozens of cottagers would crowd the wharf, mixing with Indians from the Indian Camp and those villagers who could spare the time in the busy summer months to watch the docking of the behemoths. Hundreds of passengers would disembark to mingle with the locals while mail and luggage were transferred from one boat to another. My grandfather Bartleman went almost every day, as did my relatives from the Indian Camp.

The crowds would drift over for refreshments to Whiting's Drug Store and Ice Cream Parlour, replete with marble counter, where they could also buy from a fantastic collection of bric-a-brac and tacky, cheap souvenirs, including so-called Indian artifacts, made in those days in Japan. Those with more money to spare had only to walk a few yards along the docks beyond Whiting's to shop at a variety of shoddily constructed boxlike stalls, which, incongruously, carried expensive cashmere sweaters, imported English biscuits and toffee, and embossed sportswear. Should one wish to buy groceries, there were two stores, Hanna's and Stephen's, as well as White's, a butcher shop, located in the business section not far from the locks.

In the summer of 1949 Bob and I took a steamboat trip from Port Carling to Natural Park, at the head of Little Lake Joseph. Departure was a time of great excitement. We ran to the bow of the *Sagamo*, the 744-ton flagship of the Muskoka Navigation fleet, as soon as she started to plow through the channel of the Indian River, heading for the entrance to Lake

Rosseau. We could feel the rush of fresh Muskoka air on our faces, see the smoke pour from the stack, and hear the screeching of seagulls wheeling above as they waited for the galley staff to dump their garbage overboard, as was the practice in those ecologically unfriendly days. A venerable musician who had been entertaining passengers from time immemorial (or so it seemed) started banging on a piano; the clatter of dishes being washed and coal being shovelled into the firebox rose from below decks; and the clanging of signal bells echoed from the bridge to the engine room and back.

After calling at a number of the hotels on Lake Rosseau, the captain threaded the narrow cut to Lake Joseph. We passed Redwood, where my mother had been born twenty-seven years earlier, and Yoho Island, where she had spent her early summers with her Indian parents, following a way of life the passengers of the *Sagamo* probably didn't imagine still existed in twentieth-century southern Ontario. After two hours, we entered Little Lake Joseph, the wild extension of Lake Joseph, and arrived at Natural Park. We accompanied the crowd up a steep hill to admire the view, until recalled to the *Sagamo* by sharp blasts from its whistle.

On the return trip, those who had the means ate in style in the dining room from tables covered in white linen. Bob and I gorged ourselves on junk food, precipitating an attack of seasickness during which I thought I was going to die. My mood didn't improve when a seagull decided to bomb the ship in general and me in particular; fortunately, I was wearing a hat. Sunburned and nauseated, but having undergone a Muskoka rite of passage, Bob and I were glad to disembark at Port Carling.

By the late 1950s only two steamboats, the *Sagamo* and her sister ship, the *Segwun*, were still in operation. The others had either sunk or joined the rotting hulks of previous generations of steamboats, such as the supply ship *Newminko*, which had run aground in 1942 some 200 yards from our house, and was one of my favourite places of exploration as a child.

The summer of 1958 marked the end of the steamboat era. The *Segwun* was the first of the remaining big ships to go. As it approached the docks at Port Carling from the Lake Rosseau side of the locks, an impatient crew member ordered full speed ahead when the signal to the engine room should have been full speed astern. The engineer realized that the order would lead to the ship's destruction, but he had been feuding with the crew and he poured on the steam. My father ran out of the back of the lockmaster's office as the Segwun plowed through the wooden dock. It smashed in the door to his office and came to a halt only when it met the concrete portion of the wharf, badly damaging its forepeak in the process.

The *Segwun* had only just been repaired when its inexperienced captain bumped the floating dock on the lower side of the locks so hard that the boat's propeller shaft became entangled in large chains that held the pier in place. My father donned his diving suit and eventually freed the *Segwun* by cutting the chains. The *coup de grâce* was administered when the boat was driven over shoals by an inexperienced helmsman and one of its propellers was sheared off. Taken out of service when the steamship company went bankrupt, the *Segwun* was rescued in the mid-1980s by steamboat aficionados to sail again. The *Sagamo* rotted at the dock in Gravenhurst until it burned to the waterline some years later.

The author's father with the family dogs. Wabby and Rusty hauled wood home on a sleigh and kept the village awake at night with their howling.

Eight
Nonconformists

What we need is dreamers who will stop and listen into themselves
instead of mirroring the insane scrambling which goes on about us;
who will go into the wilderness to discover new continents, not in
any unexplored or undiscovered ocean, but in the human heart and
soul.
— Frederick Philip Grove, *It Needs to be Said*

1

My father adopted the attitude that if his family was not
going to fit in, despite all his efforts, then—in a village that
valued civic decorum above all other virtues—he might as
well accentuate the eccentric. After an acquaintance told him
that he told tall stories with a flair befitting an Irish bard, he
decided to reinvent himself as an Irishman, neglecting the
small detail that his father was really a Scotsman from the
Highlands. He seized on his mother's distant Irish origins,
declaring that he was in spirit an O'Shields, not really a
Bartleman. To enhance the legitimacy of his new identity, he
purchased an "authentic" O'Shields coat of arms, nicely
embossed and ready for framing, from a mail order house
specializing in such things. He displayed it prominently on
the living room wall for all visitors to see and admire.

He erected a large sign in Gaelic on the front lawn
inviting passing Irishmen and women to stop in for a drink of
Irish whiskey; many did. He also purchased a modest out-

board motorboat, which he outfitted with a stove to keep him warm on chilly nights on the water; in this vessel he would visit the watering holes in the remaining grand old hotels on the lakes. In honour of Ireland, he installed a jerry-built forecastle, painted it green, and decorated it with shamrocks. Our house was soon festooned with Irish drinking mugs, shillelaghs, shamrocks, and other paraphernalia, as my father's newfound Irish friends reciprocated his hospitality with small gifts of their own. To cap it all, he added two enormous Arkansas donkeys to his equine menagerie; for more than a decade, he gave free cart rides to the children of the village— telling everyone the donkeys were from Ireland, of course.

I followed in my father's footsteps. It was one of my household duties, for example, to cut the grass in the spring and summer and shovel the snow off the path to our front door in winter. But I never did. Grass, weeds, wildflowers, and the occasional sapling flourished around our house, providing a nice contrast to the neatly manicured lawns of our neighbours. In winter, the path to our front door was turned into a steep slide, easy to descend if one was athletic but difficult to climb, since there were no footholds. Visitors were often forced to crawl up the steps with a rope I had helpfully tied to the front porch. Needless to say, these arrangements did not help social intercourse, and would certainly have been an obstacle to social climbing had that been our ambition.

We also kept two ferocious malamute sled dogs, named Wabby and Rusty, chained on long leads behind our house and used them in winter to haul firewood home from the bush and to take us ice-fishing. Our dogs were well known in the village for their truly astonishing howling. Once a month, with the advent of the full moon, they would throw their heads back and entertain the villagers for most of the night with a display of poetic wailing that would have put wolves to shame. The Bartlemans loved to listen to their monthly dirges; I would sometimes stimulate them to ever higher levels of performance by howling along with them. Our sense of musical appreciation was not shared by all of our neighbours; indeed, several ladies told us that the call of the wild was so forlorn that often, overcome by the sadness of the lament, they would go to sleep in tears.

Wabby was so powerful that he often broke his chains and escaped to hunt down other dogs in the village. He never lost a fight, even when he took on dogs much larger than himself. He knew when to use his shoulder, when to tear off an ear, when to mount on his hind feet to battle like a boxer, and when to crunch an opponent's leg. He never harmed humans, and had his own code of honour, disdaining to fight the smaller dogs that sometimes came out to challenge him. No one complained, since the right of dogs to fight formed part of the unwritten law of the village. Some of the villagers even acquired huge dogs of their own in the hope that their champions would be able to best Wabby, but none was up to it.

Our neighbours were less understanding when Wabby started to steal chickens. Fed on offal obtained free of charge from the village butcher shops, our dogs developed a particular fondness for fresh chicken. Wabby was not one to deny himself the occasional treat if I failed to deliver the requisite supply of chicken heads and innards; he would simply break his chains and raid chicken houses throughout the village. A considerate dog, he would always deposit a chicken on our doorstep for our own dinner after one of his forays, perhaps to make amends for his antisocial behaviour.

I loved Wabby dearly, as only a child with a favourite pet is capable. He was still alive when I went off to university. He reciprocated my affection, but to a somewhat lesser degree, once biting me in the face—an accident, I always said, but it left a scar.

2

In an attempt to inculcate a sense of responsibility in her two sons at an early age, my mother found us jobs raking leaves, painting, and doing rough maintenance work at summer cottages. One year I worked at a local grocery store stocking the shelves and ensuring that the fruit and vegetable section was well supplied. When the store was suddenly destroyed by fire, I was, at first, consumed by guilt. A great lover of bananas, I had devoured enormous quantities of them, and had developed the ability to eat one in two swallows and toss the skin into a secret location in the rafters without the owner of the store seeing me. My immediate thought on hearing of the fire was that spontaneous combustion caused by an accumulation of rotting banana skins had been the cause. I was relieved when I learned that a lightning strike during a thunderstorm was to blame.

At the age of fifteen I was hired by a tree surgeon and landscaper as his assistant for the summer months. Although afraid of heights, I forced myself to scale trees to prune dead branches and learned how to lay cement and flagstone walkways. I also obtained a weekend job, which I kept for many years, working for the local municipality helping to burn brush, dynamite rocks and stumps, and dig ditches. I became, in effect, the valiant if unofficial deputy to the village foreman. He was always in good humour and had a ready supply of jokes.

His judgment was another matter. He once borrowed

the work boat of a friend and took it out on Lake Rosseau without checking the gas supply. A vicious storm came up, the boat ran out of gas and was washed up on the rocks. It took a party of villagers and one boy (me) two days working in the rain to free it. Another time, he and I were working at the bottom of a hill behind the municipal building. The hand-brake on his truck, which he had parked on the top of the hill, failed, and it careened toward us out of control. I ran for my life and got out of the way. The foreman ran in the other direction and tried to stop the truck by sticking his leg in the way of the front wheel. He was sent reeling back, bruised and lucky to be alive.

The foreman was an excellent hunter, and he usually managed to bag a deer each fall on one of the islands on Lake Rosseau. One year he invited me to join him and his good friends, the village postmaster and a local farmer, for a day of hunting on Tobin Island, one of the larger islands on the lake. We were not dissuaded by a lack of licences; the season hadn't started, and hunting was forbidden in this region anyway. Neither were we discouraged by the absence of vocal chords in Flash, the foreman's hunting dog. The foreman proposed doing the necessary barking and howling himself, if and when Flash caught the scent of a deer.

At the island, we disembarked at the dock of a summer resident who had long since closed his cottage for the season. The foreman knew from prior reconnaissance that there were deer on the island, trapped since the previous winter and waiting for the water to freeze to escape to the mainland. He aligned us 100 metres apart along a so-called "runway"—the path normally taken by the deer—and circled around behind with Flash on a leash to drive them toward us.

About an hour later I heard the foreman howling and

barking. I readied my 12-gauge shotgun, loaded with number-one shot—more than adequate to bring down big game. The sound of human barking came closer and closer. I was filled with excitement. How proud my parents would be when I came home with a deer I had shot myself! Suddenly the foreman came into view, his howling now taking on a note of desperation. He and Flash, held tightly on a leash, came right up to me.

"Why didn't you shoot? We drove it right by you!"

My three hunting partners have long since passed away, but my sense of disgrace remains to this day. We returned to the mainland in silence. It was at this time that I began to suspect I might need glasses. I decided I wasn't cut out to be a hunter, and persuaded myself that hunting was morally wrong in principle and cruel to boot. Bob didn't wait for me to change my mind; without asking me, he traded my shotgun for a used wristwatch, which he gave to me, and a pistol, which he kept. I never went hunting again, but I wonder whether I would have adopted my newfound principles had I returned home a hero, with a winter's supply of venison.

3

It was at this time that my poor eyesight caused a brawl at the Port Carling arena. Imagine the scene. It is mid-winter and almost the entire village population has come out to cheer on the local hockey team. Normally staid citizens stamp their feet to keep warm in the minus-20-degree temperature, trampling on discarded orange peels, apple cores, and wrappers from gum and cigarette packages. Steam from their breath intermingles with smoke from cigarettes, cigars, and pipes as they hurl insults at the players from the opposing team and their supporters. The game being played is hockey in theory only. The real sport is gladiator combat on ice with every player ready to punch, gouge, butt, bite, and otherwise commit mayhem on individuals who are otherwise the best of friends. Each side, of course, has its champion. The Port Carling hero is a red-haired giant, gentle off the ice, but a demon on skates. He has already slammed several opposing players with trademark killer bodychecks but has not yet taken on the hulking, muscle-bound "enforcer" of the opposing team. The crowd is becoming impatient. There has been no fighting; this is not what they have paid good money to see.

Suddenly there is a crisis. The goal judge, perched in a crow's nest box twenty feet above the visitors net scrambles down his ladder and disappears without a word in the direction of the outdoor privy. I take it upon myself to fill in and climb up to replace him. The referee, satisfied that a competent goal judge is in place, drops the puck at centre ice. Port Carling wins the faceoff and five players surge forward. I hear the smack of a slapshot and the roar of the crowd. Peering downwards, I discover, to my horror, that I cannot see the puck. In fact, the scene on the ice below is one large indistinct mess in my myopic vision. I take an executive decision, close my eyes and switch on the green light to award a goal to Port Carling. The ensuing pandemonium indicates that I may have been somewhat hasty. It seems that the roar of the crowd was unrelated to the scoring of a goal. Once awarded, however, the Port Carling team, backed up by its non-partisan fans, was prepared to defend their unexpected goal to the death.

The two champions are soon locked in battle. The goalies, undeterred by their heavy pads, throw their hockey sticks to one side and lumber forward to clash at centre ice. Reinforcements pour in from the opposing benches. Everyone is now happy. I quietly crawl down the ladder and go home, uncertain whether the crowd thought my actions were based on design or incompetence.

4

Meanwhile, life carried on and I was thinking of girls. The dream of every red-blooded boy of my age at the Port Carling Continuation School was to find a girlfriend from among the large-bosomed, dark-haired, sexy-looking girls from the hamlet of Minette, some fifteen kilometres up a side road on Lake Rosseau. In our imaginations, they were waiting, licentiously, just for us. Every morning a yellow bus would drop off its load of students at our school, but every afternoon it would haul them away, leaving our collective tongues hanging out. I resolved to obtain a driver's licence and buy a car as soon as I turned sixteen in order to access these riches.

Shortly after my birthday, accompanied by my sceptical brother Bob, who had tried to teach me to drive, I appeared at the home of the genial local taxi driver, who was responsible for issuing drivers' permits. He assumed that I, like most boys in the village, had been driving trucks and cars long before reaching the legal age. He simply asked me to fill out the proper forms and handed me my licence before taking me out for my driver's test. With Bob in the back seat wearing a knowing smile and the examiner beside me, I meandered down the road, not seeing people and other cars until the last minute, and stalling the car whenever I tried to change gears; I still had not yet come to terms with my need for glasses. The examiner spent a good deal of his time ducking under the dashboard, but gritted his teeth and said not a word. I was clearly a threat to public safety, but he let me keep my licence.

With licence in pocket and Bob as technical advisor, I visited a car lot in Bracebridge. I had saved 150 dollars and was determined to buy myself a muscle car to impress the girls from Minette. Unfortunately, 150 dollars could only buy a 1939 Chevrolet, which was older than I was and had seen better days. The salesman assured me the motor still had a lot of life left in it. He was right as far as the motor was concerned.

What he did not mention (and what my technical advisor didn't detect) was that neither low gear nor reverse was working; nor was the choke. Moreover, the starter collapsed after we got the vehicle home. To start the car, I had first to siphon gas from the tank and spit it into the carburetor, and then quickly run to the front of the car to crank the motor until it roared into life. My problems were not yet over. I had to ensure the car was always parked on a hill, so that it would roll forward until it acquired enough momentum to proceed in second gear. Likewise, I could turn the car around only by driving it up a hill to a driveway at some strategic location and then allow the vehicle to roll backwards under the force of gravity while I, my head out of the window, turned the steering wheel in the appropriate direction.

The car was thus a total failure as far as its primary mission was concerned. No girl from Minette (or, for that matter, from anywhere else) was interested in getting into a car with a sixteen-year-old who could not see where he was going, who smelled of gasoline, whose hands were covered with grease from a hand crank, and whose success at turning the vehicle around was dependent on the availability of a strategically placed hill. All hope disappeared when the front axle broke, bringing the car to a shuddering halt and marooning it on a hill on the main street. The proprietor of the village garage tried to fix it by welding the broken parts together, but miscalculated the measurements. After I got the car back, my "muscle car" shook violently whenever I exceeded fifty kilometres an hour.

Soon after I bought my car the Minette school board decided to transfer its students to the Bracebridge high school, ending my contact, however platonic, with the girls of Minette. I sold my car for five dollars to a friend, who never paid me, and gave up trying to chase girls until I went off to university.

Nine
Metamorphoses

I hate to see that evening sun go down.
> — W.C. Handy, "The Saint Louis Blues"

1

As the 1950s became the 1960s, fewer Indians returned to
pass the summers at the Indian Camp. Lake trout, the princi-
pal fish for food and for sale to tourists, became inedible as a
result of mercury poisoning. The displays of fancywork on
the counters in the open windows of the unpainted shacks,
the smell of lake trout and bannock cooking on outdoor fires,
and the array of canoes and outboard motorboats pulled up
on the shore disappeared. Older people passed away; their
children and grandchildren found jobs in the white man's
world that provided greater security than fishing, trapping,
and making fancywork to sell to tourists. A number, such as
the late Arthur Shilling, whose work now hangs in museums
across Canada, started using their artistic talents to supply a
wider market. The disused frame houses gradually fell into
ruin and were torn down.

I inwardly mourned the departure of the Indians,
because I was losing a window on a people and culture that
formed part of my being, but I never discussed the matter
with my family or friends. My feelings were too ambivalent. I
was proud of my Indian ancestry and would never have
denied my roots. Port Carling was, however, a small commu-

Robert Clause, who gave the author a chance for higher education, and Mrs. Clause at the entrance to their Pennsylvania home in 1940. Photo courtesy Nancy Muse.

nity, and my classmates knew I was Native. I assumed, perhaps unfairly, that they shared the prejudices of their parents; an attempt at dialogue, I thought, would only provoke confrontation and embarrassment. I could well have been wrong. My classmates elected me president of our small student council several years in a row.

I suspect that people exposed to racial prejudice never get over it. Despite good relations with my classmates, I never felt that I fully belonged. As a result, I became determined to accept people as they were, warts and all, without regard for their social or racial status.

I once smuggled a bottle of whisky into the local hospital in response to the pleas of a white alcoholic acquaintance my father's age, who was about to undergo some minor surgical procedure. I knew that the hospital authorities would be furious if they discovered their patient (destined to die on the streets of Toronto) drinking, and that whisky was bad for his health. However, he had been kind to me in the past, hiring me to help him with his caretaking duties at various tourist cottages, and I felt an obligation to him that was in conflict with that owed to society at large.

It was the week before Christmas and I was sitting with my friend, when several classmates, full of good will and charity, entered the ward to sing carols to the patients. The old alcoholic turned his back on them as they burst into a rendition of "O Holy Night" and greedily sucked on the bottle, his false teeth in a glass of water at his bedside. I remained silent and unsmiling in response to the good-natured greetings of my companions from school, unhappy and uneasy that they had discovered an aspect of my private life kept hidden from them.

Not feeling in my heart that I was a legitimate member of the Port Carling white world, I used to dream about moving to Mnjikaning and being accepted as a band member. I would see myself arriving at my long-dead Indian grandfather's house to tell him, alive in my dream, that I was coming home. He would smile at me and gradually fade from view as I slowly realized that this was just a fantasy. With a white father, I would never have the right to live on the reserve or be part of the community.[13] Like half-breeds everywhere, I thought that I would always be an Aboriginal without a home, condemned to share Indian grievances against white society and to understand white attitudes to Indians.

The last Native people I was to have close relations with in those years were friends of my parents who had moved to Port Carling in the 1950s and were trying to build a life for themselves in the village. The husband had been wild in his youth, drinking more than was good for him and ending up at a prison farm in northwestern Ontario for stealing a car. One of the few prisoners ever to escape from this institution, he walked more than 600 kilometres to his reserve through the clouds of blackflies and mosquitoes that normally drove fugitives back to their jail. His father, afraid that he would be injured in a confrontation with the police who were trying to recapture him, eventually turned him in.

The couple were frequent guests at our home, where they felt comfortable speaking Chippewa with my mother. He had become an expert checkers player in prison and I never managed to defeat him in the hundreds of games we played over the years. An excellent fisherman as well, he confided in me his secret fishing spots and provided me with idiot-proof instructions on how to make respectable catches. He built a comfortable house on the fringes of the Indian Camp, obtained a steady job working as assistant to my father at the locks, and was well on his way to a stable life. One evening he decided to fell one of the giant white pines on his property. It came down on the main power and telephone lines, plunging the village into darkness and cutting off communications with the outside world. Even worse, it interrupted the evening television viewing of the villagers. In addition to community opprobrium, the family was handed a huge bill for damages, which broke them financially. The husband resumed drinking, ended up on Toronto's skid row, and died shortly thereafter.

I maintained more enduring links with my irrepressible uncles from Mnjikaning over the years, although close relations were strained by their drunken antics. On one visit to our home during my high school years, one thoroughly inebriated uncle slammed his car into my 1939 Chevrolet, which was parked on the side of the road, then staggered out with a lopsided grin, expecting me to laugh at the good fun. He eventually killed someone and was sent to prison for drunken driving. My mother laid down the law, telling her brothers that they were never to come to our home if they had been drinking. They visited less frequently, but telephoned regularly to talk in Chippewa to my mother, for whom they had enormous respect.

In later years, when they had settled down and controlled their alcoholism, my brother, sisters, and I were able to develop much closer relations with them. They were enormously proud of their nephew, keeping a scrapbook of local press stories commenting on my postings to exotic places, and sending me sweetgrass and small quill baskets at the time of my marriage and other major events in my life. One uncle even signed over a building lot on the reserve in case my sisters or I should ever like to move there. They died in the mid-1990s, still relatively young, as happens to many Aboriginal people.

2

Meanwhile, I got my big break. The caretaker for a wealthy American who maintained an estate on Black Forest Island on Lake Joseph offered me a summer job. My Indian grandfather had held the job decades earlier and had often taken the owner, a wonderful old gentleman named Robert Clause (and his father before him), on fishing expeditions. My father had also worked there for some summers before taking up his new position at the locks. I had spent a summer on Black Forest when I was only thirteen as a live-in babysitter for one of Mr. Clause's grandchildren. Although I felt that we were repeating, in Muskoka, the traditions of the antebellum American South, where jobs were passed down from generation to generation, the pay was good and I knew the family, so I accepted.

I remained there for seven summers, cutting grass, gardening, painting, chopping firewood, and preparing boats for storage. The owners arrived each spring in their company aircraft, accompanied by an Irish cook and household help, the first black people I had ever met. The Clause family were unfailingly courteous, and never condescending. They kept up a busy social schedule with their millionaire friends from the United States who maintained similar establishments throughout the Muskoka Lakes, particularly at the so-called "Millionaire's Row," at Beaumaris on Lake Muskoka.

In the spring of 1958 I finished grade twelve, the final year offered at the Port Carling Continuation School. I thought my prospects of obtaining higher education were dim. My immediate plans were to finish high school in Bracebridge and find some way to become an elementary school teacher even though my heart was not in it. On my last morning, I sat outside on the front steps with my fellow students waiting for the final class of the year to begin and the report cards to be handed out. I could not get the mournful version of the "Saint Louis Blues" as played by Louis Armstrong out of my mind. I looked at the faces of the classmates with whom I had gone to school for twelve years, certain I would not see most of them ever again. This turned out to be the case, although I was not yet through with Muskoka.

I was working that summer, as usual, on Black Forest Island, when one day Mr. Clause asked to see me on the front veranda of the family compound. The request was unusual, since my contacts with the head of the family had been confined to a respectful greeting each morning when I entered the living room to light the fire. Mr. Clause, sipping his ever-present glass of Scotch, told me in his kindly, rasping American voice that he had been giving some thought to my future. The caretaker had told him I was a reasonably good student. Would I be interested in obtaining a higher education? If so, he would finance me through the same fund he had set up to provide for the educational needs of his grandchildren. He offered to pay the costs for me to attend the high school of my choice to obtain my senior matriculation (grade thirteen) and then go on to university if I made it through this last year of high school.

After stammering out my thanks, I stumbled off the porch, my mind numb. I suddenly realized that I could become anything I wanted to be—historian, lawyer, or even diplomat. I had no idea whether I had the aptitude or the intelligence for such professions, but I had the blind confidence of youth. No challenge was now too great. I remember walking back in a daze to where I had been cutting wood, staring at huge white cumulus clouds in a deep blue Muskoka sky and listening to the lapping of Lake Joseph water on the shore of that deserted part of the island, wondering—why me?

I was to have that same sensation some years afterwards, when I opened an envelope from the then Civil Service Commission offering me a job as a foreign service officer in the Department of External Affairs, and years later when I was nominated for the first time to be a Canadian ambassador.

3

With my mother's encouragement and her promise to supplement Mr. Clause's financial assistance, I accepted his offer and departed for London, Ontario, where I rented an apartment; my Bartleman grandparents, welcoming the opportunity to escape Port Carling for the winter, moved in with me. I attended a high school, which had one of the best records in the province in turning out graduates. I did reasonably well academically and moved up the road the following year to attend the University of Western Ontario, enrolling in the four-year Honours History program.

I hated the high school and loved the university, but each played its own critical role in permitting me to escape my self-constructed Muskoka prison. London, even though it was only a medium-sized Canadian city, was a giant metropolis to someone who had spent his life in a northern community so small that it didn't even merit a traffic light. The normal Friday evening crowds of shoppers were menacing. Using the public transport system and finding my way around the city were intimidating. I had never imagined that I could be so homesick; I longed to return to the embrace of my family and to the familiar surroundings of my village. I may not have liked my place in the Port Carling hierarchy, but it was familiar and I had established my niche within it.

The high school was terrifying. Students crowded the halls, and they all seemed to know each other. Every twenty-eight minutes bells rang, and a mass of humanity moved like automatons to different classrooms to meet different teachers. The contrast to the small Port Carling Continuation School with its total complement of thirty-five students for all four grades, two teachers, and two rooms, could not have been greater. It was hard to make friends. Many of my classmates were the offspring of the North London establishment and had known each other from childhood. A country bumpkin from Muskoka, especially one who was inherently shy, was beyond the pale.

Two weeks after I arrived I fled to Port Carling for the weekend, hitchhiking north out of the city along the provincial highway, which wandered from town to town in those days before superhighways were built. I arrived in Bracebridge at three in the morning and walked throughout the night, reaching home by early morning. My mother was happy to see me, but concerned that I would not return to school. Bob, unemployed, irritable, and resentful that I seemed to be getting all the breaks in life, greeted me roughly. My father, busy brewing up a fresh supply of homemade wine, paid no attention. I called one of my friends, who had dropped out of school some years before; we spent Saturday driving around aimlessly in his car while I decided whether I would stay in Port Carling or try to make it in the big city.

Emotionally, I had an overwhelming longing to remain; in my mind, I knew I had to return. I took to the road early Sunday morning and was back in my apartment late the same day. Gradually, I established a group of acquaintances, and found that I could keep up academically with the others. After that, I returned to Port Carling only during the Christmas and Easter holidays. I had overcome what is still one of the greatest obstacles facing young people, white and Aboriginal, who come from small northern communities: adjusting to alienation in urban environments.

University was liberating. I had made the transition from village to city the previous year, and having successfully passed my grade thirteen examinations, I did not fear the academic challenge. I had not felt so free of inhibitions since the summer of 1946, when our family had arrived to start our new life on the Dump Road in Port Carling. Psychological defence mechanisms that had been developed over the years to cope with life as a half-breed in a small white community fell away. I threw myself into the search for a liberal education, paying heed to the philosophical musings of one of my professors on the first day of classes that the true function of a university was to facilitate learning through the encounter of a student with books. Formal courses or marks, he said, did not matter.

I took his advice literally. While it may have meant neglecting my course work, I learned a great deal by slipping into the classes of professors lecturing on global, religious, and ethical issues. I became a member of the History, United Nations, and Social Services clubs, and fully profited from the opportunity to meet students from Africa, Asia, and Europe. I sat in on music appreciation classes and spent long periods in the library, immersing myself in literature and history. It was here that a lifelong love for Tolstoy and Camus began.

My education also started regarding the attitudes of Canadians, outside of the small community of my boyhood, toward Native people. I quickly became aware that even in a university setting, where liberal thinking prevailed, mainstream Canadians were uncomfortable with Indians. In the late 1950s and early 1960s, when I was at university, few Native Canadians completed high school, and even fewer attended institutions of higher learning. As far as I could tell, there were no Aboriginal students other than myself at Western at that time and few students or faculty members had ever met an Indian. Their knowledge of Canada's Aboriginal reality came, intellectually, from their history courses if they were in the Humanities; their personal contact came from driving through slum-like reserves in southern Ontario, or from seeing skid-row drunks staggering from one beer parlour to another in downtown London.

I received an early shock when one of my professors offhandedly told our seminar class in Modern European History that all French-speaking Quebeckers had some Indian blood as a result of mixing with Aboriginal peoples during centuries of fur trading; that was the reason, he said, Quebeckers were so backward. I should have protested but didn't, not because I was afraid of antagonizing someone who would decide the level of my grade, but because I was discouraged. The embrace accorded to other cultures at university, it seemed, didn't extend to Canada's Native community.

I was to encounter the same facile prejudice in my subsequent careers as high school teacher and diplomat. In the teachers' staff room of the southwestern Ontario high school where I taught for a short time, before joining the Department of External Affairs, I once silenced an animated Indian-bashing session by identifying myself as an Aboriginal Canadian.

Several years later, in the foreign service, I did the same when colleagues made deprecating comments about Indians during a cross-Canada familiarization tour. A number had been hastening every evening to the local beer parlours in the north, not to drink but to amuse themselves watching Indians, some from local residential schools, get drunk and fight among themselves; one officer even went out prowling to pick up drunken Indian girls to seduce. When I was high commissioner to Cyprus in the 1980s, I spoiled a very nice dinner party in honour of the Canadian minister of defence by stopping the Canadian hostess from pursuing an anti-Indian tirade.

4

I returned to Port Carling each summer, commuting to work every day to work for Mr. Clause at Black Forest Island while living at home. My father, scarcely able to believe that one of his children had graduated from high school, much less was in university, boasted about the accomplishments of his son to anyone who would listen, embellishing my qualities and downplaying my deficiencies. Always seeking female admirers, he sought to live vicariously, chatting up local waitresses and trying to arrange dates for me.

For Bob, my annual return home brought mixed feelings. He was strongly protective of his younger brother, but interpreted that as giving him the right to pummel me at leisure—something I resisted. He once threw me through the upstairs banister and down the stairs; at other times, the furniture in our house suffered as we battled with our fists in the living room. I usually lost in these encounters (Bob outweighed me by fifty pounds), and sometimes thought of giving it all up and leaving home to avoid the constant brawling. My path rarely crossed with those of my sisters in those days. Janet, less fortunate than I, with no benefactor, obtained a job as a babysitter in Toronto to finance her studies to be an office worker. Mary finished high school in Bracebridge, trained as a nurse at the Parry Sound hospital, and returned to marry her childhood sweetheart and settle down in nearby Beaumaris.

I only occasionally came into contact with the middle-class world I encountered at university, and never felt comfortable when I was included in the social events of acquaintances whose parents owned cottages on the Muskoka Lakes. I simply didn't fit in. This was brought home when a friend from university, who happened to be the daughter of one of Canada's wealthiest businessmen, insisted that I spend the weekend at her family's Muskoka estate. The parents were openly hostile, assuming that I was out to marry the daughter and become rich overnight. I saw her again several days later as the family yacht, complete of course with uniformed crew, transited the locks at Port Carling. Neither she nor her parents replied to my greeting. She called me later the same day to say that her family had threatened to disinherit her if she even so much as spoke to me again. Associating with someone from a different class was bad enough; going out with a half-breed was unthinkable. I laughed the matter off, considering that the incident demonstrated social mores more befitting Jane Austen's eighteenth-century Britain than twentieth-century Canada.

During these summers my speech would relax back into a comfortable idiom marked by poor grammar and heavily laced with Muskoka slang. I re-established ties with Jerry and other village friends who had dropped out of school years before to join the local workforce as electricians, carpenters, or bricklayers. We played softball every evening after work. An indifferent player, I was manager, and thus assured a slot on the team as pitcher. Our team was unbeatable in our first season against the neighbouring communities of Bala and Mactier. Having unbounded faith in the prowess of Port Carling athletes, I enrolled the team the following summer in a higher league, which included Bracebridge, Gravenhurst, and the Beaver Creek Correctional Facility. We did not win a game. The Bracebridge and Gravenhurst teams beat us fairly, but the Correctional Facility (actually a medium-security jail) imported ringers from the Kingston penitentiary to ensure their victory.

The following years we restricted our efforts to playing softball with the staffs of nearby tourist resorts and, in the process, tried to attract girls. I had by this time acquired glasses and was less of a menace on the roads. My mother had bought me a 1949 Ford with leather seats and a stereo radio, not a muscle car but sufficient to permit a reasonable social life. The problem was that the starter would function only when it was grounded by a metal connection to the battery while the ignition key was turned on. Fortunately, I had a number-nine golf iron with a wooden handle that did the job in my skilled hands, albeit with a mighty shower of sparks each time.

Many of the girls working on what we locals called the "Mop Brigade," cleaning rooms and serving in the dining rooms in nearby tourist lodges, were so desperate to escape their remote dormitories that they were prepared to put up with the locals (even with my ingenious manner of starting my car), as long as we transported them to the bright lights of Bracebridge from time to time.

Once, a friend and I showed up at a dormitory determined to renew our acquaintance with several girls, who soon profoundly regretted ever having met us. The only response to our yelling and honking from the road was silence—unsurprising, since it was two in the morning; our former friends were probably hiding their heads in shame as we called for them to come out. In frustration, we decided to wash out the building; we unravelled a long firehose, turned on the water to full pressure, and systematically soaked each room and its occupants. Big-city girls were not permitted to impugn the honour of Muskoka lads!

There was no reaction to our assault, and I became worried. Perhaps the girls and the resort owner might misunderstand our motives, and consider that we were lowlife louts rather than local boys having a bit of healthy fun! What if the police were called? What would Mr. Clause think? I heaved the hose down, forgetting to turn off the tap, and called to my friend to follow me. We ran to my car, which sprang to life with the aid of my nine iron after an anxious moment or two, and sped off at high speed toward Port Carling. On the way we passed a police cruiser, hurtling with lights flashing toward the scene of our misdemeanours. No one in the dormitory revealed our names.

5

At this time Port Carling was undergoing a transformation, and not for the better. It was five years after the disappearance of the steamboats, and the public docks and locks were quiet. The elementary school and the continuation school stood empty—high school students were now being shipped to the school in Bracebridge, and elementary students to a new regional school eight kilometres away. Even the corporate identity of the village had disappeared; Port Carling was now only the name of a locality within the new Township of Muskoka Lakes. The old business centre had been eviscerated: Whiting's and the shops at the public docks had been torn down when business dried up and their owners could not meet tough new standards for septic systems; Stephen's grocery store would soon be demolished and dozens of mature maple trees sacrificed to permit the widening of the main street. Even the restaurant overlooking the river would be pulled down to make way for a new bridge.

It would be years before the process of renewal began; it would involve the emergence of an upmarket business centre, catering to a new type of Port Carling resident, drawn from cottagers who were starting to winterize their dwellings and make the village their permanent home. The closing of the school would have its positive side, exposing village youth to perspectives broader than they would have experienced if they had remained within the narrow confines of the Port Carling school. Now they would socialize with children from other Muskoka communities, including young Mohawks from the Wahta First Nation.

In the hiatus between the certainties of the 1950s and those of the 1970s, when the village would come to terms with its role within the larger Muskoka world, the puritan ethos of Port Carling was shaken to its core by the arrival from Buffalo of a band determined to make its fortune playing rhythm and blues to an affluent clientele. Installing themselves in an abandoned nightclub that had been used for more than a decade to store boats, the musicians attracted hundreds of young people to their dances from all over the lakes. The village fathers were horrified when street fights after performances among drunken young cottagers became commonplace, and when a vibrant bootlegging business developed on the side. They were even more scandalized when young villagers started to hang out with the musicians and affected a liking for their lifestyle. My father, as usual, could not resist becoming involved, befriending the manager of the group and incurring the disapproval of other members of the community.

I liked rhythm and blues and enjoyed attending the dances, if only for the atmosphere. I much preferred, however, taking in performances of the Big Bands from the United States, who were enjoying their last pre-rock'n'roll gasp of popularity. My father was given free tickets to dances at Dunn's Pavilion in the neighbouring community of Bala on Lake Muskoka in exchange for allowing advertising to be posted on government property in Port Carling. I used these tickets frequently during these Muskoka summers to listen to great musicians such as Duke Ellington, the Dorsey Brothers, and Louis Armstrong.

At the spring 1963 graduation ceremonies at Western, I mentioned this to one of my history professors, an American citizen, who told me that he was a personal friend of "Satchmo." The professor and his wife enthusiastically accepted my invitation to visit Muskoka that summer and take in a performance by Louis Armstrong. After a meal at the Bartlemans', during which we proudly showed them the new room that had been added to our house (and my father told them the story of his life), I took them to Bala. The granddaughter of my American benefactor formed part of that group that met the famous musician.

Louis Armstrong remembered the professor and gave us a warm welcome, inviting us to join him and his band, the

"All Stars," for a surreptitious drink in the intimacy of their smoke-filled tour bus during a break in the performance. We walked across a lot littered with cigarette butts and empty pop bottles to a parking area. We joined Satchmo and the other members of the band, who were sitting inside quietly in the dark, smoking and passing around bourbon whiskey hidden in a brown paper bag to avoid the attention of the Ontario Provincial Police, who would have frowned on the consumption of alcoholic beverages in a motor vehicle. Our host insisted that we share the bourbon. We drank straight from the bottle, delicately wiping the lip before passing it on to the next communicant. The professor took innumerable pictures and kept up a constant chatter. Satchmo mopped the sweat from his forehead and laughed in a good-natured way as he engaged in a spirited discussion.

I was the only Canadian present. The others talked among themselves about matters that meant little to me, with the easy intimacy and self-confidence that distinguishes Americans from Canadians. They intended no offense, and I did not take any. I sat quietly, the sounds of revelry drifting in from the nearby dance hall and "The Saint Louis Blues," played just before the break, still echoing in my ears. Listening to the hum of conversation, savouring the taste of the bourbon, soaking in the hot, humid night air, I thought of my Indian grandfather and Sam Williams from my Indian Camp days, who had died leaving no mark in history. Louis Armstrong, like them, had suffered from poverty and racial discrimination; like them, he was a man of great personal dignity and humanity. His musical gifts and qualities of his personality had permitted him to escape the ghetto and become a legend.

In my diplomatic career Louis Armstrong would be my benchmark whenever I met political leaders, who for better or worse helped shape history, and tried to determine the basis of their charisma. In most cases, I was their observer rather than their confidant. They received me and I was able to study them, not through any intrinsic merit on my part, but because I would come calling either as a diplomatic emissary on a special mission, a note-taker for the prime minister, or as an ambassador to their country accredited by the Queen. I quickly learned that political leaders had no monopoly on virtue, either in their personal or public lives. Only those who combined genius with simplicity and dignity, however, deserved to be called "great." Nelson Mandela was probably the greatest of the great. Others, whose hands I was obliged to shake in the line of duty, such as the Chinese leader responsible for the repression of democratic demonstrations on Tiananmen Square in 1989, or the Zairian president who bled his country dry for almost forty years, had the blood of thousands on their hands.

I would have the closest, if sometimes stormy, ties with Bangladeshi Prime Minister Sheik Mujibur Rahman, Cuban President Fidel Castro, and Israeli Defence Minister (and later prime minister) Yitzak Rabin, as I served as a Canadian diplomat accredited to their governments at different times in the 1970s and 1980s. I called on them frequently to make representations on human rights and other issues as necessary. All three were heroic figures in the unfolding history of their countries, with reputations and influence spreading beyond the borders of their nation states.

Sheik Mujibur Rahman, the leader of the Bangladeshi freedom fighters who helped drive the Pakistani army out of East Bengal in the civil war of 1971, was prime minister of his new country when I opened Canada's first diplomatic mission there in 1972. He always had time to meet with me and any other diplomat who wanted to see the founding father of Bangladesh in person. Like Louis Armstrong, he radiated charisma. Whereas Satchmo held one captive with his music, the sheik could hold the masses in the palm of his hand with his spellbinding oratory. I have never before nor since attended political rallies attended by millions of people who responded to oratorical direction like a symphony orchestra to its conductor, roaring approval or shouting condemnation.

In person, he was a man of quiet dignity and personal kindness. Like President Mandela, long years in prison had not embittered him. He would take me for walks showing me his favourite pets. He, of course, never mentioned the corruption he tolerated by members of his new government nor the rapes and robberies indulged in by the armed wing of his political party on the minority community defeated in the recent civil war. The people who loved him in 1972 would turn against him in 1975 and the armed forces would kill him. His military bodyguards saluted as an assassination squad of soldiers rolled into the grounds of his residence one evening in June of that year. The soldiers shot him, his wife, those family members unlucky enough to be at home, guests, servants and even the animals in his private zoo.

No one could have been less like Louis Armstrong than Fidel Castro or Yitzhak Rabin, fierce practitioners of realpolitik after decades of war and revolutionary struggle. Castro often came to the Canadian residence in Havana when I was ambassador to Cuba in the early 1980s and talked until dawn as if Marie-Jeanne and I were a crowd of 100,000 people, a *cohiba* cigar in one hand and a glass of Chivas Regal whisky in the other. He liked humanity more in the abstract than in the flesh and never mentioned the hundreds killed in summary executions after he came to power nor the thousands still imprisoned for "political" crimes more than two decades later. The Cuban commander-in-chief was at the height of his physical and oratorical powers. His hair was still black, his body armour under his shirt discreet, and his military uniform, with one star on the shoulder, always impeccably pressed. An Uzi pistol machine gun, the ultimate in fashionable self-defence weaponry was kept at the ready on the back seat of his black luxury Soviet Ziv limousine.

Fidel Castro was, however, more than a fashion plate. His charisma came from an appeal to the downtrodden, from intellectual genius, ruthlessness, a sense of history, and an ability to outmanoeuvre American and Soviet superpowers alike. I renewed my acquaintance with him in the mid-1990s only to receive a tongue-lashing for daring to suggest, on instructions from the Canadian government, that it was time for him to ease up the pressure against political dissent and adopt democratic reforms. His hair was by that time grey and his uniform no longer a tight fashion fit, but his eyes still blazed with revolutionary fire. My first impression was that he had become an old worn-out lion. I discovered, however, after twelve hours of all-night discussions, that despite his age, he still had more stamina and fire in his belly than most leaders on the contemporary international scene.

The same could be said of Yitzhak Rabin, who was Israeli defence minister in Israel during the Intifada of the late 1980s when I was ambassador to Israel. He later served as prime minister in the mid-1990s when I was diplomatic advisor to Prime Minister Chrétien. Though possessing a dominant charismatic personality, Rabin was no orator. He delivered his speeches in a dull monotone fashion and spoke to crowds as if he were delivering a lecture to a group of military cadets. His charisma came from his reputation as a warrior in all of Israel's wars and his toughness in dealing with opposition. In contrast to Shimon Peres (prime minister in the mid-1980s), who made an effort to be friendly with diplomats accredited to Israel, Rabin was barely polite. He could not stand small talk and reacted angrily whenever, on instructions, I discussed the specifics of Canada's foreign policy with him. When I protested about his edict that Israeli troops beat prisoners with clubs, he threw me out of his office.

He was a different man when I met him again in the mid-1990s over dinner in Ottawa — I was a note-taker, not his chief interlocutor — and again at a meeting at the United Nations in New York two weeks before he was assassinated. He gave no indication that he knew me despite our dozens of meetings in Israel but managed a wan smile, something he had never provided before. He was also a convert to the cause of establishing peace with the Palestinians and confident, as was the rest of the world, that a resolution to the conflict between Israelis and Palestinians was imminent.

However, the "greatest" people I would meet in my career would, in fact, not be charismatic leaders such as Rahman, Castro and Rabin, whose legacies were compromised by their need to take decisions in which lives were lost for the sake of their national causes. Rather, my heroes would be "ordinary" people like Louis Armstrong who shared their special gifts with the world. Or individuals carrying out heroic missions: a nun in Bogota who had abandoned her religious calling to work with street children; an elderly but dedicated Canadian, head of a small private aid organization, travelling on the Megna River by sailboat to bring aid to isolated Bangladeshi widows; Cuban dissidents, desperate to get their story out, risking years of imprisonment simply by meeting with me; individual Palestinians and Israelis, anxiously trying to forge bonds to move the peace process ahead, aware that they were bucking age-old centrifugal forces; and an Aborigine leader promoting healing and reconciliation, softly crying over dinner as she conveyed the trauma, keenly felt fifty years later, of being torn from her mother's arms, never to see her again, as part of a plan to turn black people into "white" Australians.

The opposite side of the coin was also true, which I discovered when I made the mistake of asking "ordinary" people what role they had played in the wars of their countries. I was startled when a heavily epauletted aide to the president of Bangladesh chuckled as he told me how he had avoided paying an individual who helped him escape his prisoner-of-war camp by simply killing him once he reached safety. Years later in Cuba, our next-door neighbour, a "family man" whose children played with ours, visited our home to have a social drink. He proudly described his role in fighting counter-revolutionaries in the 1960s, recounting his pleasure when "traitors," some as young as thirteen, would fall out of trees after he sprayed the branches with AK-47 automatic weapon fire.

6

I returned to Western in the fall of 1963 with funding from Mr. Clause and a scholarship from the Ontario government to do graduate work in history. However, I dropped out when the History Department insisted I do my master's thesis on an obscure aspect of American industrial relations rather than on my preferred topic in nineteenth-century British imperial history. The dean of Graduate Studies summoned me to his office in November 1963 and was in the process of telling me

I would never come to any good when a secretary interrupted to say that President John Kennedy had just been shot. Overcome with emotion, the dean halted his harangue, forgot to ask me to repay the scholarship money I had already spent, and dismissed me, saying I should not count on him for a reference.

I thought of that day thirty-four years later when I accompanied the prime minister on an official visit to Washington. The lodgings of the official Canadian party, in Blair House, were outfitted with furniture of past American presidents. The housekeeper showed me to my room and proudly informed me the bed I would sleep in that night was the very one in which President Eisenhower had died. After official talks and a gala dinner at the White House, we visited Arlington National Cemetery to pay our respects to the memory of President John Kennedy, passing before several thousand troops in ceremonial garb. I thought to myself that I had lived a charmed life, and that I had come full circle from that day of professorial recrimination in November 1963.

I left Western with mixed feelings. On the one hand, I felt I had let down my family and Mr. Clause, who had nurtured such high expectations of me. On the other hand, I now intended to fulfil my ambition to see the world. A career could wait until I had become mature enough to know what I really wanted to do for the rest of my life. I had been interested in foreign travel and foreign affairs from my childhood days, in part as a result of listening to my father wax eloquent on world developments and bemoan having been washed up on the shores of the remote hamlet of Port Carling and saddled with a large and quarrelsome family that had no understanding of the free life of a hobo he had enjoyed before his marriage. My grandfather Bartleman, who was castigated by my grandmother every day of his married life for all manner of mostly imaginary failings, dreamt of what life would have been like if he had only emigrated to Australia rather than to Canada, and had married someone else. As his grandson, I was his confidant. As my grandfather, he was my advisor, urging me to escape the confinements of village life.

I returned to Port Carling in the fall of 1963 to announce to my parents that I had quit university and intended to find a job to pay for a one-way ticket to Europe. I had heard that a construction company was hiring truck drivers in northern Ontario, and I was going there to try my luck. For the first and last time in my life, my father gave his opinion about my future; he said that I was acting irresponsibly, throwing the fruits of years of study out the window. Besides, what made me think I would be able to handle a truck when I had problems enough driving a car? Taken aback, I decided that if I could not be a truck driver, I would try to be a high school teacher.

From among the numerous positions available at the time, I accepted a job at a high school in southwestern Ontario, and by the spring of 1964 I had saved enough money to buy a ticket to Europe. Even though I had been an incompetent teacher, the school administration thought I had latent talent; they offered me a contract with a substantial raise if I would return for the 1965-1966 academic year. I accepted and departed on a Poor Man's Grand Tour of Europe.

The author travelling in Europe in 1964, a time of liberation from his Muskoka past and preparation for 35 years in the Foreign Service.

Ten
The Grand Tour

The joy of wandering is slow to pall, and it is to be enjoyed at the full when a man shakes himself free of all aids but his native powers and marches forth alone into the world.
— Archibald MacMechan, *The Life of a Little College*

1

I was to learn more in my one year in Europe than at any other time before or since; it was the key formative period of my life. The first lesson the fates dealt was the fallibility of human nature. A travelling companion absconded with my tickets and money, leaving me in London in the first week of July 1964 with only 200 dollars of my original stake of 650 dollars. To save money, I pitched a tent at the Crystal Palace campgrounds and began exploring travel options that would fit my straitened circumstances. I was consoled, to some extent, by the realization that I was living in a tent on the very site the *showda* of my Indian grandmother had visited during Queen Victoria's Diamond Jubilee at the turn of the century; the difference was that, as a guest of the Queen, he had a room in a hotel, whereas I was living in a tent, Native-style. I decided to adopt a Native theme for my first explorations, and spend the summer visiting Lapland, home of the Sami in northern Scandinavia.

Everything was new. Everything was an adventure. I relished the train trip to the port of Newcastle. I found the thirty-hour ferry ride to Stavanger on Norway's western coast fascinating. The youth hostels I lodged in as I hitchhiked northward were filled with other young travellers, from Germany, the United Kingdom, Australia, Denmark, Sweden, and France. Norwegians, in those days before oil transformed their country into one of the richest in the world, had a standard of living lower than Canada's, but the people were generous and welcoming. I was often invited to their homes for meals, and every effort was made to squeeze me into their small overloaded vehicles.

Norwegians and the young people I met from throughout Europe were just as interested in knowing about Canada and me personally as I was in learning about them, their families, and their countries. With some hesitation, I described my mixed roots. To my surprise, I discovered that on the other side of the Atlantic, Indians were regarded as courageous, warrior-like, and endowed with an inherent ability to commune with nature, as well as victims of brutal colonial aggression. Exposure to the romantic notion of the noble savage, which goes back to Jean-Jacques Rousseau in the eighteenth century, and to Karl May's depictions of the heroic exploits of Native Americans in popular literature at the beginning of the twentieth century, had left its mark. Europeans had a positive picture of Indians that was as stereotypical and as much out of touch with reality as was the opposite image held by white Canadians. I preferred the European perspective, so I didn't mention the wild parties on Saturday nights at the Indian Camp, or the antics of my uncles.

As I went farther north, I became aware that Norway was much larger and longer than I had imagined. I discovered that it was as far from Oslo to Hammerfest on Norway's north coast as it was from Oslo to Rome. I persevered even when it rained every day and my money supply began to dwindle.

Fortunately, I had brought with me Tolstoy's *War and Peace*, and did not mind standing in the rain for hours, reading while waiting for lifts. I reread the 1,500-page masterpiece twice, thumbing with difficulty through the sodden pages, and killed countless mosquitoes; after five weeks, I found myself at Tromsö, above the Arctic Circle, where, to my surprise, the road ended.

To celebrate, I decided to have a drink in a local bar. Unfortunately, one drink led to another. Then several Norwegian sailors insisted on buying me a drink; of course, my Muskoka honour obliged me to return the favour. When it came time to pay the bill, I discovered that in Norway alcoholic drinks were prohibitively expensive. I had blown almost all of what remained of my budget and I had not yet met any Lapps.

I had to find a job to finance my return to London. A fellow traveller told me that the fish factory at Hammerfest, still some hundreds of kilometres north along the coast, was hiring workers and paying good wages. Without hesitation, I spent most of my remaining funds on a ticket for the next boat. I boarded the ship at seven in the evening and travelled all night under the midnight sun; my fellow passengers included German tourists and local people returning to their fishing villages along the coast. We arrived in Hammerfest in the early hours of the morning. I found a town recently rebuilt after being razed to the ground by retreating German soldiers at the end of the Second World War, a few sleepy residents, no Lapps, several dozen reindeer browsing contentedly on the village square, and the fish factory—which had just closed for the summer holidays.

With no prospect of employment, I decided to make my way to Helsinki, 1,200 miles away and the closest capital city with a Canadian embassy to which I could appeal for help. Blueberries were abundant. Perhaps I could hitchhike to Finland and live off the land like my Indian ancestors; I might even meet Lapps.

I set off, packsack on back, *War and Peace* in hand, and fifteen dollars in pocket. Unfortunately, while there was a dirt road leading to the Finnish border, there were few people and even fewer cars. I stood on the road for days, usually in the rain, and slept on the side of the road. Every day I ate blueberries for breakfast, lunch, and dinner. The only protein I received was from the giant mosquitoes that came down in clouds and were ingested with the blueberries. My hands, my mouth, my lips, my tongue, and other parts of my body that I will not describe turned purple. Fortunately I did not grow tired of blueberries; I looked forward to my browsing each day. Perhaps it's a genetic gift.

Eventually I arrived at Karajok, on the Finnish border, where to my delight I discovered a community of Lapps. They were dressed in traditional costumes, did not speak English, and were not interested in communicating with me by means of sign language. They had seen too many anthropologists.

I crossed into Finland and made my way southward to Rovaniemi, on the Arctic Circle, where I parted with two dollars and spent the night in a hostel for men—an experience not to be repeated. I was directed to a room filled with double-decker bunk beds and given a place among two hundred unemployed lumberjacks. At midnight, I awoke moaning and crying uncontrollably. Everyone else in the room seemed to be doing the same. I was participating in a type of collective unconscious hysteria, probably brought on by one person having a nightmare and infecting others with his melancholy mood. Or perhaps it was just northern madness. I did not sleep the rest of the night and left as soon as I could the next morning.

Unfortunately, knowing no Finnish, and being unfamiliar with Finnish ways, I mistakenly stopped a taxi. The driver thought I was a fare-paying passenger; I presumed he was a generous Finn helping a poor traveller on his way. After driving me some distance, he began to suspect I could not pay and I started to realize that the ride was a commercial affair. Our parting was difficult, with my packsack heaved onto the road and many arm and fist gestures in my direction. I did not need a translator.

I was more careful before accepting future rides. As I made my way south, there were more people and more cars. As in Norway, the locals were generous—perhaps too generous. One couple insisted on putting me up at their summer house near Kuopio, which is Finland's tourist area closest in character to Muskoka. Unlike in Muskoka, however, the Finns expect their visitors to share their saunas. I had no objection in principle; after all, the only real baths I had had for weeks came from the rain. So I found myself sitting naked with strangers, female and male, as they poured water on red-hot rocks, beat themselves with birch branches, and then ran naked to jump into the ice-cold lake. I lost my tan, and my lungs burned for days from inhaling steam.

At Helsinki I went to the Canadian Embassy to seek help. A beautiful French-Canadian vice-consul, who exuded sex and sophistication, listened to my sad tale; she told me the Canadian government would not advance funds, but offered to send a telegram to my mother for help. I decided at that moment that the foreign service was really for me and that it was time to learn French.

My mother sent me one hundred dollars, not quite enough to buy a railway ticket to London. I took to the road once again, hitchhiking to the Finnish port of Turku, where I boarded a ferry for Sundsvoll across the Gulf of Bothnia in Sweden, and then I was on the road again to Stockholm. There were no vacancies at the Stockholm Youth Hostel; I walked past the dining room windows of the Grand Hotel, the most elegant (and expensive) hotel in the city, and watched prosperous Swedes and tourists fork rich food into their mouths and down glasses of fine French wine. The night I passed in the central park, falling asleep to the voice of Paul Anka, then at the height of his popularity, who was performing at a nearby public concert. I awoke with water pouring into my sleeping bag from a sudden storm, and fled at three in the morning to the main railway station, to await dawn and the departure of a train for London.

I was not to see Scandinavia again until thirty years later, when I returned as Canadian ambassador to NATO in 1994 to observe military exercises along the Norwegian coast north of Tromsö, and later accompanied the Canadian foreign minister to a meeting in Oslo. As Canada's ambassador to the European Union, I returned again in June 2001, this time to Stockholm, to attend a summit meeting between Prime Minister Chrétien and the presidents of the European Union and the European Commission. The Canadian delegation was accommodated at the Grand Hotel, and I found myself eating in the dining room that overlooked the sidewalk I had walked down thirty-seven years earlier. Fortunately, there were no hungry backpackers outside to stare at me as I shovelled down my bourgeois food and savoured my excellent French wine.

2

In London I purchased a copy of *The Times Educational Supplement* and applied to two different schools for a teaching position. As was my wont, I demonstrated an unerring instinct for the wrong choice. The job I rejected was at a grammar school in Oxford teaching O level—roughly equivalent to Grade 12—history. I was not too sure what a grammar school was but thought that the quality of the students could not be high if they still had to be taught grammar at the high school level. Instead, I chose to accept an offer from a Secondary Modern High School at Leigh-on-Sea in Essex, reasoning that since it was "modern" and "secondary" I could not go wrong.

What a mistake. Middle-class parents dropped well-dressed students off at the entrance to the school each morning in their cars (the teachers came to school on bicycles). These adolescents, I discovered, were poorly motivated and academically weak. They did not have high enough marks to enter grammar school. I had to hand out school-books and pencils before each class and collect them afterwards, or the students would lose them. They laughed at my accent and, despite frequent applications of the cane by the headmaster, had a level of discipline that would have disgraced their opposite numbers at the Port Carling Continuation School.

Here I encountered for the first and only time in my life an avowed sado-masochist. Hearing prolonged screaming from an adjacent classroom, I opened the door to see a dementedly smiling fellow teacher standing over a student lying on the floor, with one foot on his back and two hands twisting his arm. When he saw me my colleague released the arm, which remained frozen in the air as he came to greet me.

Later, in the staff room, which appeared to be the place where such matters were discussed, he told me he enjoyed inflicting pain; thus teaching, he claimed, was for him a satisfying profession.

The British teachers I met welcomed me, but I never adapted to the British teaching culture. The school was coeducational, but in name only; one section was reserved for girls and the other for boys, and no mixing was permitted. At lunch, the sexes shared one large cafeteria, but fraternizing was not allowed. Teachers ate at one long table, but men sat at one end and women at the other. I caused an uproar when I suggested to some of my fellow male teachers that we take our plates and join the ladies.

Unable to endure teaching at the Essex school, I returned to London, where I was hired (at a higher salary) as a hall porter at the British Council's Overseas Student Centre in Portland Place. The job could not have been more satisfying. While the British themselves were standoffish, I became friends with a wide variety of university students and *au pair* girls (students learning English and earning their keep by doing light housekeeping chores) from the continent. I rented a two-room flat close to Baron's Court Underground for the equivalent of about five dollars a week and lived very well. Canada House became my real home away from home—the place where I picked up my mail, read outdated Canadian newspapers preoccupied with political scandals and the debate over the introduction of the new Canadian flag, and met other young Canadians doing their thing in London. Occasionally I caught sight of a Canadian diplomat (in those days indistinguishable in London from their British counterparts) carrying a black umbrella and wearing a bowler hat, hurrying to a pub lunch.

My fellow hall porters were war veterans, Irishmen who introduced me to Guinness draft beer, which remains my favourite. My responsibilities were confined largely to checking identities at the door and directing people to the toilets. Several years later I was able to use these senior responsibilities to good effect when I submitted a curriculum vitae to support my foreign service application, noting with just a touch of exaggeration that I had been an information official at the prestigious British Council in London, England, at one time in my brief career.

The kindly librarian at the Council made free tickets available for concerts at the Albert Hall and Festival Hall, and for other major cultural events in the British capital. I would rush off almost every evening to listen to the best symphony orchestras and the most gifted pianists; on weekends, I would take in the art galleries. It would have been a heady time for anyone, let alone for someone from a small rural community in central Ontario.

I even picked up a few pointers on how to pass the examination to become a foreign service officer. Each week I attended lectures on governance at the British Council by senior British politicians and civil servants. One British diplomat described in a self-important way how he had prepared himself for the British Foreign Office examinations and interviews many years before: he had learned to be knowledgeable but not a know-all; to be sensitive but not emotional; and to like poetry but not let it show. I filed this information away for future reference.

The Second World War had been over for nineteen years, and change was in the air. Newspapers were full of stories reporting that Britain, the ostensible winner of the war, was falling farther and farther behind the countries on the continent, whose economies had been destroyed two decades previously. To my surprise, one could still see vacant lots where bombed-out buildings had once stood. There was much soul-searching over the loss of empire. The death of T.S. Eliot, the great poet and playwright, was a sign that the generation that had fought in the Great War was passing. Winston Churchill's death was the definitive signal that an era had ended. Accompanied by a Finnish sculptor and two Swedish *au pair* girls, I stood in line for five hours outside Westminster Hall to file by his coffin and pay my respects. The next day I joined hundreds of thousands of Londoners on the route of his funeral cortège. Never in all my years in Canada's diplomatic service have I seen such pomp and circumstance as when Britain said farewell to its greatest twentieth-century hero.

In London I was also to have a foretaste of the great ferment that was occurring in the United States, which would in short order bring about the desegregation of the American South. Earlier in the year, while working as a teacher to purchase my airfare to Europe, I had travelled with my father to visit my sister Janet, who was living with her American serviceman husband on an air force base in Montgomery, Alabama. The United States South of that period was truly an alien and sinister place to me; I felt deeply uncomfortable at the sight of segregated restaurants, barbershops, and rest rooms in the racially divided towns and villages that we passed through, and wondered where Indians would fit into this hierarchy of racial discrimination.

Passing through Birmingham, I could still see in my mind's eye the television images of "Bull" Connor, the police chief who some months earlier had set dogs and steel-helmet-ed troopers armed with batons on marching black children. In Montgomery I visited the state capital, where the era of "black awakening" had started with Rosa Park's refusal to give up her seat on a bus to a white passenger in 1955, and where "Freedom Riders" were beaten with lead pipes and baseball bats in 1961. Governor George Wallace was still an unreconstructed racist in that spring of 1964, and there was little indication, at least to me, that the region was on the verge of momentous change.

If change was to come, however, it was generally accepted that it would be led by Dr. Martin Luther King. I was thus immensely privileged to have been present at a sermon by the leader of the United States civil rights movement at Saint Paul's Cathedral in London. I had come to listen to a free organ recital in the unheated damp cathedral when the dean introduced Dr. King, who was on his way to receive the Nobel Peace Prize in Oslo. There were only twenty of us scattered here and there in the immense church, but Dr. King did not seem to care. His eyes were fixed on the back of the cathedral rather than on the congregation, and I had the impression that he was addressing history rather than us.

After Dr. King described his efforts in the civil rights campaign, he drew on the sermon he had made famous, intoning "I have a dream." He then quoted the seventeenth-century dean of Saint Paul's, John Donne: "No man is an island entire of itself; every man is a piece of the continent, a part of the main; ... never send to know for whom the bell tolls; it tolls for thee."

Dr. King, assassinated by James Earl Ray on April 4, 1968, could have been referring to himself.

3

By February 1965 I felt it was time to move on. Having travelled to the extreme north of Europe, I wanted to see the farthest south. I applied for and obtained a job teaching English at a language school in Bari, on the heel of Italy. I never made it; I stopped off en route to visit a friend in The Hague and decided to stay in the Netherlands. Her family insisted that I be their houseguest, afraid, in those days before the sexual revolution, of what might happen if I were to find separate, unsupervised accommodation.

This was my introduction to the habits and culture of the continental European bourgeoisie. The family's home was in Wassenar, one of the most exclusive neighbourhoods in the Dutch capital, if not in the entire country. The head of the family was never seen without a jacket and tie, even on weekends. The evening meal was always preceded by cocktails—invariably Dutch gin, taken straight, with *kroepoek* (a shrimp cracker) as a snack; wine was served at dinner; knives were held in the right hand and forks in the left, not constantly shifted back and forth during the meal as in North America. (No elbows on the table, no thumb on the dish, no crackers in the soup, and don't even think of licking the plate, even in jest!) The family went every week to a cultural event, usually to a performance of the magnificent Royal Concertgebouw Symphony Orchestra, and always took me along, reinforcing the introduction to classical music that had been initiated during my stay in England.

My first job was as an English teacher at an academy for foreign languages, but it was incredibly boring. At the local labour office I was offered the choice of working in a bakery or in a steel-fabricating factory; I opted to be a baker. My friend's parents seemed doubtful about my new job, but were positive, at least initially. They outfitted me in overalls, lent me a small motorbike, and sent me on my way. I returned that night exhausted and covered in flour. Instead of a small bakery making croissants and other delicacies for a discerning clientele, my place of work was actually an enormous factory that produced bread in commercial quantities. My job consisted of carrying and dumping hundred-pound bags of flour into huge revolving pots, and sweeping the floor; it did not compare with working at the British Council.

My hosts were aghast when they saw the flour on my clothes when I returned. What would the neighbours think? A worker living in Wassenar! My friend's father, head of a large Dutch insurance company, offered me a job as his private secretary with much higher pay, if I would only drop being a baker. I was unenthusiastic, since I did not know how to type and was not at all certain I liked the girl well enough to work for her father. The mother had the solution, producing an advertisement from the *International Herald Tribune:* the American International School of The Hague was urgently seeking a teacher. I telephoned, got the job, and my career as a baker came to an end.

Looking back after so many years, and having had my three children educated at American schools in different countries, I am ashamed to say that I was an irresponsible teacher. I was more interested in visiting the sights of Amsterdam, travelling with my Dutch girlfriend, and reading than in the welfare of the students. I often took my charges to the beach in the morning and left them there all day. We played baseball at every opportunity, and more than once I knocked out windows in the neighbouring Bulgarian embassy, then fled indoors with the students to avoid the ambassador's wrath.

I did, however, teach my students a few things, and in the process moved one step closer to being able to join the foreign service. Having been drilled in the fundamentals of grammar in the Port Carling Public and Continuation School, I inflicted it on my students every day until the parents complained; my students probably thank me for it today. More importantly, I purchased copies of *Time* magazine every Monday morning for each student from my relatively generous American-dollar salary. For the rest of the week we would conduct a detailed exegesis of its contents, neglecting all other subjects (except grammar) to discuss the issues of the day. When I wrote the foreign service exams to enter the Department of External Affairs in Canada one year later, no one was better informed than I on world developments; the examiners must have thought I was a genius.

4

During the three-week Easter holidays I made one final major trip before bracing myself to return to the reality of making a living in Canada. Still wishing to get to Bari, I stationed myself on the highway leading south from the Dutch capital, determined to hitchhike to the southern toe of Italy. A car pulled up; I opened the back door and hopped in. The passenger in the front seat jumped out; the car started up. I said, "Thank you for giving me a lift." The driver said, "Who in the hell are you?"

He had stopped to let out a passenger, not to pick me up; but he decided to let me stay anyway, and became more friendly as we proceeded toward Brussels, his destination. He was knowledgeable about both Italy and Spain, and recommended that I visit Spain before the arrival of the sweeping changes that would inevitably follow the death of the dictator, Generalissimo Franco, who had come to power in the bloody civil war of the 1930s.

I thus lurched southward in the direction of Spain, rather than Italy. On the outskirts of Brussels, a young American couple stopped their car and asked if I was familiar with Belgium and northern France. They were on their way to Rheims to see the great cathedral associated with Joan of Arc. I told them I was an Honours History graduate from the University of Western Ontario. I had never been to Rheims, but directing them there and giving them a tour of the cathedral would be a mere bagatelle.

We made our way down the valley of the Meuse River toward the French border, with me describing the various fortifications and historical sites as if I really knew what I was talking about. We crossed into France and arrived in Rheims, where I took them to a big church, described its historical background, and recounted the ordeals of Joan of Arc. They took numerous photos, thanked their learned Canadian guide for his help, and went on their way. It was at that point that I realized that I had taken them to the wrong cathedral—the real one was some distance away. It was magnificent and I enjoyed visiting it, even if alone.

On leaving Rheims the next day, I saw an enormous sign inviting tourists to visit the champagne wine cellars, more than ten kilometres in length, owned by a subsidiary of a large Canadian multinational drinks company. I suspected that the invitation was meant for travellers who had money to spend, but decided to take advantage of the offer. After receiving me sceptically at first, an information officer gave me a tour lasting several hours, complete with free samples of the product. I repaid my debt many times over during the next thirty years by serving champagne from these vineyards exclusively, at all official functions where champagne was *de rigueur*. The last opportunity to do so occurred when I was ambassador to Israel, and my wife and I received the owners of the vineyards for dinner. I related my story, served their product, said thank you, considered my debt paid in full, and felt free to change.

Spain provided my first encounter with a developing country. In the absence of road traffic (few people owned cars), I purchased a twelve-dollar third-class ticket, valid for 1,200 kilometres, at a railway station not far from the French border, and headed for the British colony of Gibraltar, at the southern tip of the Hispanic peninsula. I soon found out why the ticket was so cheap. The train was crammed with garrulous Spanish peasants and their snotty-nosed children, whose hygiene left something to be desired. Strong body odour and the smell of garbage poured from the compartments, and the passengers spat on the floor and blew their noses with their fingers whenever the urge struck them. My fellow travellers did not speak English and in those days I did not speak Spanish. The fact that communication was limited did not matter; being in a police state, they were suspicious of strangers in any case.

The train travelled at an average of twenty kilometres an hour and stopped at every hamlet on the way. I tried to travel twenty-four hours a day when possible, aware that I had only a limited time before my Easter holidays would be over. At times it would pull into a railway siding in a remote community and all the passengers would be herded off to sleep in cheap hotels near the railway station while the crew took on coal and water for the locomotive. I fell into a deep sleep during one of these stops and dreamed I could hear the staccato opening beats of Beethoven's Fifth Symphony, repeating themselves with growing intensity. I awoke in the pitch-black night to hear someone knocking with four insistent hammer blows on each door, the sound growing in ferocity as it approached my room, summoning the passengers to take their places on the train. Half asleep and clutching my possessions, I staggered into the pale artificial light of the station platform to board the train, which was about to continue its snail-paced journey across the vast highland plateau.

The passengers quickly fell asleep on the hard wooden benches that served as seats, many with their mouths open, some snoring. I was reminded of the scene from *Wind, Sand and Stars* in which the author, Antoine de Saint-Exupéry, travelling by train in the 1920s, watches the faces of sleeping Polish immigrant miners returning to their homeland from France and wonders who from among that mass of apparently brute humanity could be the next Chopin, if only he or she had the opportunity. I remained awake to catch the first light of the day and to watch the sun rise over the neighbouring mesas.

We eventually descended onto the hot Andalusian plain, where it was possible to pick oranges from trees beside the track from the windows of the slow-moving train, and arrived at Algeciras, the Spanish city at the crossing point to Gibraltar. In those days, Spain's dispute with the United Kingdom over the ownership of Gibraltar was in one of its periodic crises; on my return to Algeciras from Gibraltar, the Spanish border guards emptied my suitcase on the ground to punish me for consorting with their enemy, but let me re-enter Spain.

By a stroke of luck, I met an American tourist who was on his way to Zurich in a rented car. I offered to show him Spain, in return for a free ride. He welcomed my offer, not knowing that I knew no more about Spain than he did. I promptly took him to Portugal, which I had always wanted to see. He seemed so happy with my guiding efforts that I then took him to Madrid, where we visited the El Greco masterpieces at the Prado and took in a bullfight. I rooted for the bull, which, against the odds, gored a matador, before being dispatched by a sword thrust to the spine. At this point my American host began to have doubts about my sense of direction; assuming responsibility for the navigation, he drove over the Pyrenees into France and from there to Switzerland.

I was not to see Spain again until I travelled with Marie-Jeanne to the World's Fair in Seville in 1993, as a guest of the Spanish government. I returned again with Prime Minister Chrétien as his foreign policy advisor in July 1997, to attend a summit meeting of NATO leaders, during which the Canadian and Spanish prime ministers made every effort to put the 1995 confrontation over fish in the North Atlantic behind them. Franco had been dead for a generation, and Spain had become a prosperous, democratic member of NATO and of the European Union, rivalling Canada in the size of its gross domestic product. Gone for good were the impoverished peasants, the outdated infrastructure, and the pervasive climate of fear and suspicion of a police state.

5

My gap year in Europe over, it was time to return to Canada. I said goodbye to my Dutch friends and departed for Prestwick, Scotland, to take a Trans-Canada Airlines flight to Gander, Newfoundland. Aware that my time for uninhibited travel and exploration was coming to an end, I decided to hitchhike from Gander to Muskoka, persuading myself that I needed to complement my newly acquired knowledge of Europe with a glimpse of life as seen from the open road in Atlantic Canada.

The weather was glorious and the people welcoming, that June of 1964, as I made my way to Port Carling, the village of my boyhood and youth. The Trans-Canada Highway from St. John's to Port au Basques, on the south coast of Newfoundland, my immediate destination, had just been built, and there were few cars and trucks on the road. However, I had little trouble in obtaining lifts; even if they were going in the opposite direction, people would turn around to help me on my way, or they would offer to take me home for a meal. In Corner Brook, where I spent the night trying to sleep in the railway station, good-natured local veterans waiting for a train insisted that I join them as they drank and sang their regimental songs.

After crossing by ferry to North Sydney, Cape Breton Island, I followed the Trans-Canada Highway into New Brunswick, where I spent an entire day standing on the side of the road waiting for a ride, eventually becoming so desperately thirsty that I stopped a passing farmer on a tractor to beg a drink of water. That night I slept in the dense brush beside the highway, and was eaten alive by mosquitoes and blackflies. The next day, when I crossed into Quebec, I was struck by the profusion of Canadian maple leaf flags being flown from houses as well as from businesses. I was proud of the new flag, but (not having fully understood the debate over its adoption, which, *inter alia*, had pitted Francophones against Anglophones) was puzzled as to why I had not seen the same expression of patriotism in Newfoundland and New

Brunswick.

The same evening, a truck driver on his way to Montreal picked me up. I fought to stay awake, aware of the unwritten code of the road that obliged hitchhikers to make conversation and provide company. I could not keep my part of the bargain; my head would droop and my body pitch forward as I fell into a deep sleep. I would awaken with a start and jerk back into my seat, only to collapse again, restarting the cycle. In the seconds of deep sleep I snatched when I lurched forward, strange visions came to me. I cried out as scenes from the twelve months spent in Europe flashed in graphic colour before my eyes. Fact mixed with fiction as my brain sought to integrate the experiences of other cultures into the world view I had taken with me on departing for Europe one year previously. The driver looked relieved when he dropped me off in Montreal at dawn.

I returned to a Port Carling that had not changed since I left; it still mourned its days of glory, when the Indians came back in the summers and the steamboats put the village on the map. My grandparents were still alive, and they joined my parents, my brother, and my two sisters in according me a hero's welcome. My parents then accompanied me to a tavern in a neighbouring "wet" community to celebrate the return of the son who had braved the wilds of Europe and Eastern Canada to come back to his family and village.

I then left Port Carling for good and, after fulfilling my obligation to teach at my southwestern Ontario school during the 1965-1966 academic year, passed the exams to join the Department of External Affairs. Port Carling, however, never left me. The young man about to embark on a diplomatic career in July 1966 was not, of course, the half-breed child who had arrived in Port Carling nineteen years previously as part of a family that was starting at the bottom of the Muskoka socio-economic and racial hierarchy. I had changed and so had Port Carling.

That change would continue. I would learn other languages, become familiar with other cultures, marry a non-Canadian, raise a family abroad, and represent Canada on five continents, in a career lasting more than thirty-five years. Other people—the sons and daughters of the villagers of my youth and new arrivals, few of whom I would recognize when I returned periodically to visit my family—would populate the community. The time had long passed when I should have been able to rid myself of the demons of my Muskoka youth and move on. They were too powerful, however, and I found it impossible to come to terms with the village life that had shaped my being. The consequence was that in my own mind I remained an outsider, with an uncertain identity in Canadian society.

It was thus a defining moment of my life when, in 1985, the antiquated law denying Indian rights to the children of Indian mothers and white men was changed. With my brother and sisters I was granted Indian status, and we were accepted as members of the Mnjikaning First Nation, with a right to live at Mnjikaning or the Indian Camp should we so wish. When I was accepted as one of theirs by my mother's people, one of the great ambiguities of my identity was settled, and for the first time I was liberated to participate as an legitimate Aboriginal member of Canada's multicultural society.

Epilogue

When you no longer go around accounting for yourself, making yourself understood, justifying your existence, when you no longer feel alien anywhere, you've come home. You know who you are.
— Wilfred Pelletier, *No Foreign Land: The Biography of a North American Indian*

The old house in the village where I was raised has now been torn down, as has the barn and the cabin of my grandparents; the forest has reclaimed the land. My father, having outlived all his old drinking friends, lives in a nursing home dreaming of Ireland, in a world where his long-dead horses are still alive. My brother and two sisters have rediscovered their links with the people of Mnjikaning, never missing powwows and major community events. Bob travels each day by boat to his place of work as caretaker on an island on Lake Muskoka; in the evenings and on weekends, he pursues his first love, carving and making furniture. Janet moved to Oregon many years ago with her husband, who left the American Forces to join the USA Forest Fire Service, but returns to the village each fall. Mary raised a family at her home on Lake Muskoka; of all the children, she is closest to my mother. Although my mother's links with the people of Mnjikaning have remained strong, she continues to live in Port Carling, the discrimination of the early years a thing of the past.

In the interim, the First Nations of Mnjikaning and

Wahta, joint custodians of the Indian Camp in Port Carling, raised themselves by their bootstraps. The former established a marina, an industrial park and eventually a casino employing some 3,500 workers drawn largely from neighbouring communities, with the proceeds shared among more than 100,000 Native people across Ontario. The latter followed suit, embarking on a highly successful cranberry growing and tourism development ventures. With employment and prosperity, more and more people were able to replace their old houses and to send their children to institutions of higher learning where many enrolled in Native studies programs.

During these years I spent most of my life abroad, living in a time warp, stuck psychologically in post-war small town Ontario, with discrimination and exclusion fresh in my memory. I had long since identified myself with the Indian rather than the white part of my being. Writing this memoir has allowed me to reconcile these two parts and to come to terms with existential issues such as death, spiritual quest, and injustice. I had thought I had resolved these years before, but they re-emerged unsolved through the mental fissure broken open in the wake of the mugging in South Africa. The depression returns periodically, but the dream within a dream that plagued me over the years has, I hope, been banished forever.

Perhaps I should be grateful to my South African assailant for opening my eyes, but I am not—not yet anyway.

Notes

THIS MEMOIR IS FOUNDED ON MEMORY—voluntary and involuntary—as long-forgotten incidents from my boyhood and youth flooded in as I sought to put order into my Muskoka past. The context was enriched by my personal contacts with members of both the white and Aboriginal communities. White villagers, born in the late nineteenth century into families of the first pioneers, were more than willing to describe life in Muskoka to their inquisitive paper boy in the 1940s and 1950s. Aboriginal veterans and elders from the Indian Camp were also happy to provide accounts of their early lives.

Those interested in learning more about the early history of Muskoka might wish to consult the list of Selected Reading. I recommend, in particular, books by Richard Tately and the late Leila Cope on the white history of Port Carling. There are no books of similar quality dealing with the Aboriginal people of Muskoka – they were a forgotten people and their past a gap in the collective memory of mainstream society. There are, however, primary source documents from the National Archives which provide a glimpse into the Native presence in Muskoka. A book I have treasured for years is *Muskoka and Haliburton 1615-1875 – A Collection of Documents from the National Archives*, published by the Champlain Society and the source for many references in the memoir.

1. THE CORE OF THE PERMANENT VILLAGE population was composed of the descendants of the first settlers, mostly Protestant Ulster immigrants, lured to Muskoka in the latter half of the nineteenth century by the promise of good farmland. They got rock and bush instead. The pioneers then found alternative employment in a short-lived logging boom, during which the old-growth white pines were felled. They turned to tourism when Muskoka became the destination of choice for the well-off from southern Ontario who travelled northwards on the railroad to Muskoka Landing at Gravenhurst, where they embarked on steamships to the first of the grand hotels and cottages on the lakes.

Muskoka was discovered at the same time by wealthy Americans from the Pittsburgh area who built palatial residences on the three lakes. And then, following the Second World War, a wave of predominately middle-class Canadians rolled in to thicken the shoreline with their cottages, coexisting, but not mixing with the descendants of the wealthy patricians who had come earlier. The summer residents of the village, who in those days were not to be seen between Thanksgiving and Victoria Day, were drawn from Toronto and Hamilton and kept largely to themselves, playing golf at the Muskoka Lakes Golf and Country Club and maintaining a busy social schedule with their peers.

2. PRIME MINISTER MACKENZIE KING introduced legislation in the Canadian Parliament establishing a universal family allowance program in 1944. The first cheques were issued in 1945, providing a social security net for all poor Canadian families with children, for the first time.

3. WADSWORTH DESCRIBES MEETING "the Indian Medicine Man of the Ojibway Tribe, Named Musquedo, at Obogawanung Village, now Port Carling. He was then eighty years of age but strong and vigorous. He had a flag pole in front of his hut with an emblem on top to denote his vocation. He invited me to a White Dog Feast and other

pagan ceremonies...." Wadsworth confirmed that the community was prosperous: "When Mr. Hart and I were encamped there, Musquedo brought us potatoes and corn and we gave him pork and tobacco in return."

4. CHIEF BEGAHMEGAHBOW'S petition of 1862 to the Crown for a reserve at the site of the future Port Carling.

5. THE LAKE SIMCOE CHIPPEWAS were the descendants of the Anishinaubeg people who in the early eighteenth century moved from the lands surrounding Lakes Superior and Huron into what would later be called southern Ontario, driving out the Iroquois and establishing communities throughout the area. In those years, the Anishinaubeg maintained close links with French fur traders, missionaries, explorers, and soldiers, many of whom married or lived with Indian women.

The Anishinaubeg supported France in its ill-fated struggle against Britain for control of North America, which ended with the defeat of Montcalm by Wolfe at Quebec in 1759. Together with the Indians from throughout the Great Lakes and Ohio Valley regions, they supported the subsequent Indian uprising led by the war chief Pontiac (himself an Anishinaubeg), leading to the capture and destruction of almost all the British forts west of the Ottawa River. Mollified by a conciliatory British policy towards the Native peoples in general, the Chippewas of southern Ontario then became firm allies of Britain, welcoming onto their lands in what would become southern Ontario the United Empire Loyalists and their Mohawk allies, who had been driven out of the United States following the victory of the Thirteen Colonies in the Revolutionary War of 1773 to 1783.

The Anishinaubeg also provided the largest number of warriors to the coalition of Indian forces which fought, under the great Shawnee war chief Tecumseh, on the side of the British in the war of 1812-1814, helping save Canada from American conquest in the initial stages of the war and playing the decisive role in the capture of Detroit. Despite shabby treatment by the colonial government, which had dispossessed some of the families of the Lake Simcoe Indians of their lands in the vicinity of the future Toronto a generation earlier, some seventy warriors from the region fought with Tecumseh's forces, several of them distinguishing themselves.

6. DOUBLE STANDARDS WERE APPLIED to Indian women under Canadian law. Until 1951, Indian women were forbidden to vote in band council elections. They also had no voice in land surrender decisions. Prior to the passage of Bill C-31 in 1985, Indian women lost their Indian Status on marrying white men, and their children were denied the right to Indian status. However, Indian men who married white women retained their Indian status, and their non-Indian spouses automatically acquired the status of Indians as did their children.

7. AN ANCESTOR, CHIEF THOMAS NANEGESHKUNG, is recorded in the original petition to the lieutenant governor of Upper Canada dated July 1, 1839, dealing with the establishment of the Rama Reserve. He is recorded again in a document dated May 26, 1842, complaining to Sir Charles Bagot, governor general of British North America, that payment promised for the forced relocation of members of his people to Rama had not been made. His son, Joseph Benson Nanegeshkung, replaced him as chief in 1858.

8. THE FEDERAL FRANCHISE WAS NOT EXTENDED to all Indians until 1960; the provinces accorded the right to vote to Indians at various times from 1949 (in British Columbia) to 1969 (in Quebec). Ontario extended the franchise in 1954.

9. UNTIL THE 1960s, the Federal Department of Indian Affairs administered Indian Reserves using a system of agents to apply the provisions of the *Indian Act*.

10. THE POTAWATAMI, an Anishinaubeg people from Michigan, sought refuge with their Chippewa cousins in southern Ontario in

the nineteenth century to escape the wrath of the Americans for siding with the British in the war of 1812-1814.

11.   THE REBELLION OF 1837 was a revolt for political and economic reform against the government and a privileged group known as the Family Compact. Although it was suppressed by the militia, Mackenzie returned from exile some years later to be elected to the Legislative Assembly.

12.   THIRD SECRETARY is the most junior officer rank in the diplomacy. Second secretary, first secretary, counsellor and ambassador are the progressively higher ranks.

13.   IN 1985, with a change in the *Indian Act*, my brother, two sisters and I were accepted into the band as full members.

Selected Readings

ALLEN, Robert. *His Majesty's Indian Allies—British Indian Policy in the Defence of Canada, 1774-1815*. Toronto: Dundurn Press, 1993.

BENN, Carl. *The Iroquois in the War of 1812*. Toronto: University of Toronto Press, 1998.

COATSWORTH, E. S. *Notes on York County's Indian Background*. York Pioneer and Historical Society, 1956.

— *When Muskoka Defended Toronto*. York Pioneer and Historical Society, 1954.

— Notes on the Ojibwa (Chippewa) Indians Gathered From the Rama Ojibway Indian Reserve 1937 and 1938. Unpublished.

COOMBE, Geraldine. *Muskoka—Past and Present*. Toronto: McGraw-Hill, 1976.

COPE, Leila M. *A History of the Village of Port Carling*. Bracebridge: Herald Gazette Press, 1956.

FLOOD, Josephine. *Rock Art of the Dreamtime*. Sydney: Angus and Robertson, 1997.

JENNESS, Diamond. *The Ojibwa Indians of Parry Sound; Their Social and Religious Life*. Ottawa: Bulletin No. 78. National Museum of Canada, 1935.

KOENNESCKYE, Franz. *The History of Parry Island, An Anishnabwe Community in the Georgian Bay*. M.A. Thesis, University of Waterloo, 1984.

LEACOCK, Stephen. *Sunshine Sketches of a Little Town*. Toronto: McClelland and Stewart,1960.

MURRAY, Florence, ed. *Muskoka and Haliburton 1615-1875—A Collection of Documents*. Toronto: University of Toronto Press, 1963.

MALOUF, Amin. *On Identity*. London: The Harvill Press, 2000.

SCHAMALZ, Peter. *The Ojibwa of Southern Ontario*. Toronto: University of Toronto Press, 1991.

SMITH, Donald. *Sacred Feathers: The Reverend Peter Jones and the Mississauga Indians*. Toronto: University of Toronto Press, 1987.

SUGDEN, John. *Tecumseh, A Life*. New York, Henry Holt and Company, 1997.

TATLEY, Richard. *Port Carling—The Hub of the Muskoka Lakes*. Erin: The Boston Mills Press, 1996.

— *Steamboating in Muskoka*. Bracebridge: Muskoka Litho, 1972.

TRIGGER, Bruce, ed. Vol.15, *Handbook of North American Indians—Northeast*. Washington: Smithsonian Institution, 1979.

WASHBURN, Wilcombe, ed. Vol.4, *Handbook of North American Indians—History of Indian-White Relations*. Washington: Smithsonian Institution, 1988.

Afterword

FROM HIS EARLY DAYS in the Canadian Foreign Service, Jim Bartleman stood out as a man endowed with great abilities not only in creative thinking and intellectual analysis, but equally in action, implementation and management. That winning combination was to take him far. Combined with hard work and dedication, it launched him on a remarkable career in demanding assignments in Ottawa and abroad. Jim went on to become one of our most accomplished diplomats.

After an eclectic mix of assignments at the start of his career and the unique opportunity of establishing Canada's High Commission in Bangladesh, his first management job in Ottawa was as director of the Caribbean and Central America Relations Division. There, he produced a well-regarded policy review on Canada's ties with the region that helped prepare him for a successful tour of duty as Ambassador to Cuba, at a time when the relationship with that country commanded much high-level attention in Ottawa. He went on to become director general of Intelligence Analysis and Security and director general of Economic Intelligence.

When he accepted the always challenging job of ambassador to Israel, Jim did so well in this crisis-prone assignment that he held it for five eventful years, serving through periods of great tension. His hand on the helm was firm, his policy advice to Ottawa clear-sighted and fair, and his understanding and support helped his colleagues at the post through many difficult moments.

He moved on from Tel Aviv to Brussels, where his tenure as

Ambassador to NATO spanned major changes in post-Cold War Europe and the early days of the transformation of former adversaries into the partners of tomorrow. Jim's perspective and grasp of the broader context as well as of the immediate issues were widely noticed, and his reputation grew. It was not surprising, therefore, that Prime Minister Chrétien brought him home to be foreign policy adviser to the prime minister and assistant secretary to the Cabinet for Foreign and Defence Policy.

Jim's performance in this position became a by-word around Ottawa. He was determined to carry out to the fullest what he saw as both a mission and a privilege: to advise and support the head of our government in all his international dealings. While working closely with the prime minister and his political advisers, Jim always knew how to preserve his role as a public servant offering his best professional, nonpartisan advice. He asked to leave, after more than four years, only when he realized how badly he needed relief from the burdens of what was recognized by his peers as an all-consuming devotion to duty.

As head of mission in South Africa, Australia and to the European Union in Brussels, Jim continued to serve Canada well. His responsibilities included support for Canadian business and other private sector interests, assistance to our citizens abroad, advice to the increasing range of Ministers and Departments in the Government of Canada active in the international domain, and assistance to provincial and municipal representatives.

Jim's career has been diverse and fascinating. As an ambassador, he had the opportunity of representing his country in dealings with some of the most charismatic leaders of our time, from Fidel Castro in Cuba to Nelson Mandela in South Africa. As the Prime Minister's foreign policy adviser, he met a cross-section of the world's political leaders. Through all this, he brought to bear some of the key attributes of the country he loved and served so well:

hard work, dependability, fairness, prudence, common sense — and a great sense of humour.

It would be impossible to close this afterword without mentioning the enormous contribution made by Jim's partner in this life-long journey, his wife Marie-Jeanne. She supported him through difficult times, and she and their three children provided the focus and continuity so necessary in a life of constant disruption. Jim's family is a success story as great as his career, and bears witness to his human qualities. He is a true example of a great Canadian public servant.

— *Gaëtan Lavertu*, Deputy Minister of the Department of Foreign Affairs and External Trade

ABOUT THE COVER

The cover was designed for the press by Cindy Morriss of MORRgraphics Inc. in Ottawa. The background artwork is after a watercolour of the Bartleman home by Jean W.A. Forder (1919-2001), House at Port Carling, circa 1955, and the foreground photo of the author was taken while he was travelling through Europe in 1964. The contrast between the two pictorial elements appropriately signifies the confidence, energy, and determination that launched him on his career after leaving Muskoka.

The book was set in Palatino 11 / 13, and the captions set in R Stempel Garamond, 10 / 13 at Penumbra Press in Manotick, Ontario.

The Penumbra Press logo was designed by Carl Schaefer, OSA, RCA (1903-1995).

AUTHOR'S ROYALTIES in Canada have been assigned to the Aboriginal Achievement Foundation for scholarships for Native students.